Praise for
Human Work

"Jamie Merisotis takes concepts too often used to justify exclusion—credentials, skills, and technology—and repurposes them to provide an ambitious but pragmatic blueprint for dismantling longstanding systemic disparities. *Human Work* recognizes the true ends are not greater efficiencies and revenues, but greater equity and economic mobility. This book is required reading for anyone committed to the future success of our increasingly diverse nation."
—**Spencer Overton**, *Professor of Law, The George Washington University, and President, The Joint Center for Political and Economic Studies, America's Black Think Tank*

"Jamie Merisotis lays out a powerful argument that the rise of new technologies does not need to accelerate inequality. In fact, through the stories of workers, he shows that people, no matter their starting point, bring critical human attributes that make work personally meaningful and valuable to modern society. This book is a timely blueprint for us all."
—**Amy Liu**, *Vice President, Brookings Institution, and Co-Founder and Director of Brookings's Metropolitan Policy Program*

"Jamie Merisotis provides a fresh, timely, and relevant analysis of the complexities of human work as the world transitions into an era of uncertainty. Jamie has a unique capacity to combine deep and well-informed analysis with interesting anecdotes and observations. A must read for those committed to building a better future."
—**Francisco Marmolejo**, *Education Advisor, Qatar Foundation for Education, Health, and Community Development, and Former Global Tertiary Education Lead with the World Bank*

"This book is a refreshing alternative to sensationalistic claims that AI, robots, and automation will soon replace a majority of human workers. Merisotis presents an inclusive vision of the growing need for work that only humans can provide, with constructive steps that educators, leaders, and workers themselves can take to increase their employability and life satisfaction."
—**Ken Goldberg**, *Roboticist and William S. Floyd Jr. Distinguished Chair in Engineering, University of California, Berkeley*

"Jamie Merisotis offers a compelling vision for the future of education by calling for learning systems that prepare people for 'human work'—the work that only people can do with artificial intelligence and automation on the rise. He shows why education that cultivates human capabilities like creativity, critical analysis, empathy, and ethical reasoning is more important than ever. It's a book for our time."
—**Dan Porterfield**, *President and CEO, The Aspen Institute*

Human Work

in the Age of Smart Machines

JAMIE MERISOTIS

RosettaBooks®

NEW YORK 2020

Human Work in the Age of Smart Machines
Copyright © 2020 by Jamie Merisotis

First edition published 2020 by RosettaBooks

Cover design by Sarah Herbert
Interior design by Jay McNair

ISBN-13 (print): 978-1-9481-2262-7
ISBN-13 (ebook): 978-1-9481-2260-3

Library of Congress Cataloging-in-Publication Data

Names: Merisotis, Jamie, author.
Title: Human work : in the age of smart machines / Jamie Merisotis.
Description: First edition. | New York : RosettaBooks, 2020. | Includes
    bibliographical references and index.
Identifiers: LCCN 2020017560 (print) | LCCN 2020017561 (ebook) |
    ISBN 9781948122627 (hardcover) | ISBN 9781948122580 (ebook)
Subjects: LCSH: Human capital. | Labor supply--Effect of automation on. |
    Employees--Effect of technological innovations on. | Manpower planning.
Classification: LCC HD4904.7.M469 2020 (print) | LCC HD4904.7 (ebook) |
    DDC 331.25--dc23

www.RosettaBooks.com
Printed in Canada

RosettaBooks®

Contents

For my parents, Peter and Diana Merisotis,
who taught me that the most important part of work
is not what you earn, but what you achieve.

Prologue

"Work is a good thing for man—a good thing for his humanity—because through work man not only transforms nature, adapting it to his own needs, but he also achieves fulfilment as a human being and indeed, in a sense, becomes 'more a human being.'"
                    —Pope John Paul II, Laborum Exercens
                        (On Human Work), 1981[1]

An old saying about music goes, "Writing about music is like dancing about architecture."[2] I've felt this way a lot over the years as I've tried to write about the world of work and how we prepare people for work through learning. Much like "dancing about architecture," I wonder if writing about something as complex and nuanced as work is an almost absurd exercise. After all, billions of people around the world work, and they do so in as many ways as musicians make music.

But I continue to write about work and the development of human talent necessary to accomplish this work for a fundamental reason. Work matters. People work not only because it helps them economically but also because it offers them social mobility, personal satisfaction, and a range of other rewards that are almost impossible to describe. The technology innovator and investor Roy Bahat may have summed it up best when he said most people work not only for stability—to make money, to have a comfortable life—but for dignity. "You're part of something greater than yourself, and it connects to some broader whole."[3]

The existential threats the world faces—pandemics, global warming, and challenges to free societies—serve to remind us of our shared humanity, our desire to build and maintain relationships, and the importance of work in our lives. The emergence of COVID-19 as a public health nightmare showcased the perseverance of people who are prepared for work in an uncertain future as it underscored the need to develop coordinated approaches for readying everyone.

Work is changing in unprecedented ways as technology and artificial intelligence take over more of the tasks people used to do. The robots might or might not be coming to take our jobs, but it's clear that society is being thrust into a new era of human work: the work only humans can do in the age of smart machines. Human workers will do more than make money to support themselves throughout the rest of their lives. They will be learning, earning, and serving during the course of their lifetimes, participating in a virtuous cycle that expands human potential and allows all of us to make a difference. We'll need to prepare for this new era by developing our human capacities such as compassion, critical thinking, ethics, and interpersonal communication—in college, at work, and in our daily lives. This means we need new approaches to formal and informal learning after high school that intentionally develop human traits, while also expanding opportunities for service so people can gain greater meaning and satisfaction from life.

In my 2015 book, *America Needs Talent,* I suggested the acquisition and development of talent will drive America's future prosperity. By "talent" I mean not simply innate ability, such as being able to play a sonata or score a penalty kick, but more broadly the combination of knowledge, skills, abilities, and other capacities that are honed through learning and experience in ways that not only improve individuals, but advance society in general. Evidence from the past few years shows this talent imperative exists globally. Data from the Organisation for Economic Co-operation and Development (OECD) and individual countries show demand for talent developed through formal learning has increased more rapidly than expected. The future of work in a technology-mediated world will create even greater demands for this more fully developed talent.

This book, however, is not titled *The World Needs Talent* or *America Needs More Talent*. In the years since my last book was published, it's become apparent the dramatic changes in work are accelerating. For one thing, work is no longer synonymous with "job"—performing tasks that employers will compensate us for with wages, benefits, and professional advancement within a firm—because many people who are working are no longer in jobs. They are contractors, gig workers, people who do multiple tasks—sometimes quite different ones—to earn money. And they are blending their interests and abilities in ways we have not seen before.

To be sure, some of the changing nature of work is driven by corporate and employer demands, at times aimed less at meeting the needs of workers and more on driving results and profit. While this issue and its consequences are important, workers themselves also are staking claims to their own work futures. Rather than be defined by a job, people increasingly are defining themselves by their ability to do various kinds of work, and by their talent. And talent can be applied wherever it's needed and useful—to make a living, certainly, but also in service to others. We live in a world where many workers say jobs no longer offer the sense of purpose and meaning they once did. Survey research from Gallup shows that fewer than one-third of workers feel engaged with their jobs.[4] Yet most workers say that having real meaning in their work is essential to happiness and life satisfaction.

The social consequences of the loss of purpose and meaning through work have been greater isolation and loneliness and less social cohesion, a trend that has accelerated since political scientist Robert D. Putnam described it in his groundbreaking book *Bowling Alone* two decades ago. Indeed, Amy Goldman, CEO of GHR Foundation in Minneapolis, an innovative philanthropy reimagining what's possible in service to people and their limitless potential for good, told me she fears this trend may be indicative of an even deeper social dilemma. "The problem isn't simply that we are bowling alone," Goldman said. "It's that we aren't bowling at all."

But a talent-based world suggests an alternative in which people apply their own unique talents not only to provide for themselves and their families, but also to contribute to their communities and work toward a stronger society.

Now the age of smart machines is upon us, and the application of artificial intelligence to work—especially the repetitive tasks almost all workers do to a greater or lesser extent—will put more pressure on traditional job functions. Human work is what people must be prepared to do. At the same time, smart technology is allowing people to become passive consumers of entertainment and information, further contributing to the social isolation the elimination of millions of jobs has caused. The only possible response is to develop talent at a scale that has never been attempted.

By its nature, technology's effects are global. Unlike raw materials and industrial products, information and data move instantaneously throughout the world at virtually no cost. Their only barriers are political, and even those are harder to enforce. In the knowledge economy, a major factor driving the renegotiation of trade agreements, including the North American Free Trade Agreement and the global agreements negotiated through the World Trade Organization, is the need to reduce barriers to services and not just goods. Whether this globalization of knowledge and skills will be beneficial to individuals and nations depends on their response to it.

The economic imperative to increase talent is inextricably connected to individual well-being, to quality of life, and to the stability of democratic systems and nations. This new talent imperative means our education systems, many of which are highly localized, will need to be connected to broader efforts to match learning needs with the changing structures of work, society, and the economy.

Readers will find what follows is not the typical public policy–laden argument that is my signature. Instead, I tell the stories about today's workers and strive to speak more broadly to the issue of human work by arguing:

- Work brings shape and meaning to our lives and is not just about a job.

- As artificial intelligence ultimately leads to the automation of virtually all tasks that are repetitive or can be reduced to an algorithm, work does not go away but is transformed into the work of the future: *human work—* the work only people can do.

- Human work blends human traits such as compassion, empathy, and ethics with our developed human capabilities such as critical analysis, interpersonal communication, and creativity.

- We urgently need a large-scale, continuous system for developing and deploying quality learning that will prepare people for human work and life in this new age of smart machines. Combined with opportunities for serving others that enhance and magnify this learning, this new system will create a virtuous cycle of earning, learning, and serving others.

- The economy is rapidly becoming people-centered, which demands new and different systems for employment and learning. Both individuals and the economy depend on people developing their abilities throughout their lives and being able to match them with needs in the economy and society. This requires that everyone—employers, educators, and workers—speak the same language about what work requires and what they know and can do. In other words, the worlds of work and learning are merging into a single system based on continuous learning and credentials whose meanings are clear and transparent.

• It's not just the work of the future that requires us to develop our abilities for human work. The abilities and capabilities needed for human work are the same ones necessary to assure a more equal and just society governed through democracy.

People cannot and should not compete with machines for work. We can't prepare people for human work by trying to make them more like machines. But I also don't believe machines are becoming smarter than humans or that we're evolving into a new hybrid species—what the novelist and futurist Arthur C. Clarke called "robo sapiens." Instead, people need to focus on what makes us different from machines by developing our knowledge, skills, and abilities through a learning system that puts human capabilities and values first. Just as each of us needs to up our own game, other actors in the human work ecosystem also must do better.

Some people will no doubt argue dissolving the lines among earning, learning, and serving will be hard because existing institutions are committed to the established order. This is certainly true, as we've seen efforts to create change in each of these areas resisted by forces internal and external. But it's also true that human development has advanced to a point where we cannot have a "learning phase," a "serving phase," and an "earning phase" without significant disruption. Witness the difficulty of

the generations of workers who were engaged in hands-on manufacturing processes, such as making automobiles or producing
consumer goods, and how, after the Great Recession of 2008–10,
those jobs were obliterated at an accelerated pace.

We now know that, unlike in previous times when many jobs
would return after a recession, these jobs won't come back. "Retraining" an individual who has been ejected from an entire line
of work—a line of work the person's parents and grandparents
also may have performed—is a massive challenge. Though we
cannot give up on the retraining process, it's clear many workers
are on the cutting edge of a new reality: work and learning must
exist side by side, enhanced and enriched by service to others,
with a sort of ratcheting-up process over time to higher levels of
talent as work continues to evolve. People aren't retrained once,
but instead many times during the course of their working lives.

My efforts to contribute to the thinking on this topic may at
times feel as if I am trying to dance about the architecture of this
new world of human work. But it's worth trying, because in the
end, this new human work ecosystem will serve a noble cause—
the development of human potential to do work that makes a
difference for individuals and society.

How Work Is Being Transformed

"So often in life, things that you regard as an impediment turn out to be great good fortune."
—Ruth Bader Ginsburg[1]

Work is changing in unprecedented ways as technology and artificial intelligence take over more of the tasks people used to do. It's not simply that smart machines are doing things people cannot or will not do. It's that they are doing things *with* people to help people do what they do, as humans, better.

This is the lesson Joel Lewis learned as an assembly line worker in the American Midwest. Lewis's story is not uncommon when it comes to manufacturing jobs and robots. But unlike a lot of what's published about how robots are affecting work, his experience is not about robots replacing human workers even as robots keep getting smarter.

Lewis began working at Cummins Inc. on an assembly line, putting in ten-hour shifts stuffing pistons into diesel engines for Dodge Ram trucks. Twenty-two years later, he has seen the assembly process at the Indiana-based manufacturer of power generation and diesel engine products transformed by process innovation and new technology.

"I see change as a good thing," Lewis said. "We need to be able to work smarter, not harder."

Lewis has worked in a variety of assembly and testing roles at Cummins in plants in Columbus, Indiana, the company's corporate home, and in Seymour, about a half hour south of Columbus on Interstate 65. And he's had a lot of coworkers, including some new "colleagues" in recent years: the company calls them collaborative robots, or "cobots." They are smart machines made possible by advances in sensor technology and artificial intelligence that allow robots and human workers to share the same space—literally working side by side.

Cummins had deployed cobots in fourteen of its plants by the fall of 2019, with the objective of having the machines in nineteen factories by the end of that year. Cummins's intent is simple—to make life easier for human workers, not to get rid of them. "The whole idea is to have the robot work collaboratively with the human worker," said Elizabeth Hoegeman, the company's executive director of manufacturing engineering. The cobot, she said, is "working in the same workspace and doing things that are less appetizing to the worker."

For example, the cobot can perform any type of labor that offers ergonomic challenges, such as having a worker bend over repeatedly to pick up a box. Machines can also do work that might expose a human to potentially harmful chemicals. "Your only limitation is your imagination" when it comes to designing roles for the cobots, Hoegeman said.

Cummins consults with its factory workers to define roles for the cobots. Sometimes the workers offer suggestions for how manufacturing processes can be improved, and other times the comments are more personal, Hoegeman said. "One worker might say, 'If I don't go home with back pain, I'm happy.'" The human workers help the machines learn their functions. By taking over dull-and-dangerous repetitive tasks, cobots allow human workers to concentrate on the higher-level and more creative elements of the work.[2]

As his workplace has changed, Lewis, now in his late 40s, has gone through several phases of training and retraining. And he's also trained other workers. He said many workers are initially intimidated by the changes, but they can be persuaded the changes are worthwhile if they produce benefits for the workers.

Does Work Have a Future?

"Joel Lewis and the Cobots" sounds a bit like an ominous science fiction novel. But does Joel Lewis and his experience represent the end of work as we know it, or a new beginning?

I can't say I have read everything that's been written about the future of work, but I've read a lot.[3] It's hard not to—the topic continues to fascinate journalists, futurists, and even philosophers.[4] While the topic covers a lot of territory, many if not most of these articles and books focus on the effects technology is having on all types of jobs—not just in manufacturing—and how artificial intelligence will eliminate many of these jobs and dramatically change the rest in the near future.

Technology's advancement and the exponentially increasing capacity of computing technology have been well documented. This pace is likely to continue or even accelerate. In 2019, Google reported a true breakthrough in computing capacity using a quantum computer.[5] The speed associated with quantum computing is vital to the success of machine learning and artificial intelligence capabilities.

Artificial intelligence—AI—is indeed different from the technologies that constantly transform our society and economy. Throughout human history, from the most primitive tool to the most complex industrial robots, technology has extended the reach of what people can do. As technology advances, it has taken over countless tasks people have previously performed—just as it has done at Cummins. It always has and always will. Quantum computing is just the latest example of how technology can alter the pace of tasks in ways that were inconceivable even in the recent past.

But AI represents something new. As the name implies, AI is about thinking—the most human of activities. The automation of thinking, in the opinion of many, will change our economy and society as much as any technological shift humanity has experienced. Klaus Schwab, the economist and World Economic Forum founder, calls the period we are entering the Fourth Industrial Revolution and predicts that, as with revolutions that came before, it will disrupt work and employment for most people around the globe.[6]

Many reports about the future of work focus on the idea that vast numbers of jobs will disappear soon because of AI. Here are several of the more breathless claims:

- "Half of all U.S. jobs could be eliminated."[7]

- "Accountants have a 95% chance of losing their jobs."[8]

- "Automation threatens 800 million jobs."[9]

- Or perhaps the most extreme view: "[The claim that 99% of all jobs will be eliminated] may seem bold, and yet it's all but certain."[10]

- Even actor Martin Freeman says, "CGI in films is so advanced actors could soon be 'rubbed out.'"[11]

I could go on. The most reliable headline about the future of work is that it will include the loss of many jobs, and no one's job is safe. Indeed, some people who study the future of work have concluded we must prepare ourselves for a future *without work*, in which a universal basic income replaces employment and people do something with their lives other than work.[12]

I believe the preoccupation with job loss in much of the writing about the future of work is misplaced. These stories spin the (not very compelling) tale of a zero-sum economy. Much more complex outcomes are likely than simply "truck driving will disappear" or "everyone needs to learn how to code." Those oversimplifications mask the broader patterns at play.

No one knows how many jobs will be lost to AI. A 2018 *MIT Technology Review* analysis of all major studies about job loss and creation, from sources ranging from global consulting giant McKinsey & Company to the OECD and the Bank of England, determined "we have no idea how many jobs will actually be lost in the march of technological progress."[13] So trying to keep up with the guessing game seems to me to be largely a waste of time and effort.

Labor economists have studied the likelihood of different jobs disappearing as a result of AI and automation, and their results are revealing.[14] Job loss is not the whole story. Technology has always created jobs even as it destroys them, and in the past it has tended to create more jobs than it eliminates.[15] Technology has caused some jobs to disappear or be transformed in ways that demand new and more advanced skills, but we also know technology has created millions of new jobs for people with the requisite knowledge and skills—particularly in knowledge-intensive sectors. There is no reason to believe it will be any different this time.

The Future of Work or the Work of the Future?

Perhaps it would be better if we thought less about the future of work and more about the work of the future. In this sense, it's not helpful or correct to frame the issue as job loss. It's really about job *change* and *displacement* and how we prepare people for an inevitable future in which they need to be more flexible, adaptable, and prepared for whatever opportunities present themselves. What's more important than whether a particular job will go away is that everyone will see jobs changed in some way by technology and will need additional learning to take advantage of the opportunities for work that inevitably will be created.

Take the financial services sector. With AI and automation inexorably replacing human tasks when it comes to data analysis, many people believe "machines are becoming a threat to warm-blooded number crunchers worldwide," according to a 2019 Bloomberg analysis.[16] But job-search companies report many of the same banks and investment houses in which smart machines have supplanted human data analysts are now actively seeking people with different skills to develop stronger information systems, do ever more sophisticated data analyses, and, in effect, manage the robots. At these organizations, data scientists are in high demand.

Seth Jayson, senior analyst at the financial insights firm The Motley Fool, makes the point clearly. "Big companies in the U.S. are actually looking for liberal arts type of graduates because they want people who have a broader background than just a narrow set of skills that you might get out of finance or something else," Jayson said on a 2019 podcast. "And you can always move into the finance area from other fields. I mean, look at me. I was an art history major."[17]

Another, more concrete example of how jobs are being transformed is that of bricklayers. (Pardon the pun.) A new robotic bricklayer can lay three times the number of bricks as a skilled human worker, and, as some articles about this smart machine note, it doesn't stop for water breaks or join a labor union. But even the inventor of the robotic bricklayer says its purpose is to make better use of human workers and not replace them.[18] Bricklayers are still needed to set up and guide the machine, read blueprints, and do the more complex or tricky parts of the job, including tasks that require creative solutions.[19] The same dynamic is playing out in job after job across the world economy.

Tasks, Skills, and the Future of Work

An extensive Vanguard Research study of the forces at play is revealing.[20] Rather than focus on jobs, the researchers looked at the underlying tasks making up jobs in the top hundred occupations in the United States and classified them as basic (requiring few skills and little or no training), repetitive, or "uniquely human." The latter category includes the kind of tasks I am talking about—those requiring "an adaptability to situation and circumstance that can't be codified." This is human work that smart machines can assist with but can't take over.

Unsurprisingly, jobs made up primarily of tasks that fall into the second category, repetitive tasks, are at the greatest risk of automation. What is more interesting in the research is that the composition of tasks in occupations has changed dramatically in recent years, with a rapid increase in uniquely human tasks. A good example is the occupation of photographer, which has shifted away from repetitive technical skills such as processing film to tasks only humans can do, such as "thinking creatively" and "establishing and maintaining interpersonal relationships." This shift has been dramatic and rapid. In the case of a photographer, 80% of the tasks that make up the occupation are different from what they were in 2000. Across all occupations, half of all tasks are uniquely human, compared to just 30% of tasks in 2000. Projections of these trends suggest this number could rise to 80% in the next ten years.

Perhaps most encouraging, this research found technology is increasing the demand for people to perform human work. As technology replaces many basic tasks and tasks that can be automated, the human component of jobs becomes the key differentiator and—according to the data—the chief contributor to value. In human work, technology is a complement to what humans bring to the work, not a replacement.

But more worrying is that the emergence of human work as the main jobs driver has been accompanied by larger numbers of people dropping out of the labor market even as unemployment also declines. As human work becomes an increasingly important share of job tasks, too many people lack the necessary knowledge, skills, and abilities.

If a task is repetitive, it can be automated—this much has been clear since the first robot replaced an assembly line worker.

The jobs most likely to be lost are those that consist of a single or well-defined set of repetitive tasks.

This already has happened at a large scale. When a Subaru plant opened in Lafayette, Indiana, in 1989, a human performed nearly every weld on each of the eighty-eight cars produced there daily. By 2016, robots were doing the welding and the plant produced 1,350 cars every day. AI is now being coupled with these robots to do inspections and identify defects for quality-assurance purposes—and a whole new category of workers may see their jobs disrupted.

Jobs consisting entirely—or almost entirely—of repetitive tasks *are* at highest risk of elimination, but all jobs will be transformed as companies automate the repetitive tasks within them. At the same time, the bar for what constitutes a repetitive task is constantly shifting as artificial intelligence becomes more sophisticated.

The economist Richard Baldwin, former senior advisor to President George W. Bush and a leading expert on globalization, has described AI not as "artificial intelligence" but rather "almost intelligent."[21] We know from the field of psychology that intelligence requires reasoning, abstract thinking, and problem solving—all things that, today, are not possible with machines. Yet machines are capable of learning quickly and learning from experience. This is why tools such as Google Home and self-driving cars are advancing so rapidly.

This innovation suggests that, when it comes to work, not only manual tasks can be automated. A lot of work that relies on expertise and knowledge can be analyzed and reduced to algorithms that can be applied to specific problems through automation. We always thought the distinction between low-skilled versus high-skilled workers was all-important. But now we know it doesn't matter so much. If a task is repetitive, even if it requires a high level of skill, it potentially can be automated. If jobs mostly consist of these repetitive tasks, they are at risk.

Some jobs comprising repetitive tasks are low skilled, but not all. After all, the welders making Subaru cars and trucks were highly skilled, but that didn't mean the tasks they performed could not be automated. What AI does to jobs is extend the reach of automation beyond manual tasks. Even highly skilled professionals such as lawyers, accountants, and surgeons can see their jobs threatened if all they do is apply their knowledge and skills—no matter how sophisticated—to common or consistent tasks. On the other hand, some jobs we usually consider low skilled, such as food servers, will remain, even as others in the same industry, such as cashiers, will likely disappear.

This asymmetry within and across industry and job classification suggests being prepared for the work of the future involves applied skills. But this is clearly not the whole story. Not all tasks can be automated, and not all jobs can be replaced by smart machines. Simply put, not all work is repetitive, although some days it feels this way for too many of us. This nonrepetitive work—the work machines cannot do—is what we need to focus on.

So much of how we think about work and jobs is wrong. We still argue about whether we place too much emphasis on white-collar jobs, and whether more people should be encouraged to enter blue-collar jobs. For most of the 20th century, even most of the postwar period, this two-track approach was workable, and even generally correct. Most Americans quite accurately saw themselves as destined for one of two career paths: pursue a college degree (typically a bachelor's) or learn a trade.

These days, though—as in just about everything, it seems—the norms no longer apply. The "either-or" approach to education and training is still clear and simple, of course—it's easily understood. But it's patently wrong. Not just morally wrong because of the inherently unjust sorting mechanism it creates, but factually wrong.

Careers simply don't work like this anymore. Few of today's workers hold jobs that resemble the blue-collar work their parents might have done. Technology is too pervasive, the need for higher-level skills such as communication, teamwork, and critical thinking too strong, for any job not to require some type of college-level learning. Career preparation no longer is adequately defined by the college-or-not choice.

Instead, what seems to be emerging is a vast gray area, a fluid, ever-expanding workspace that includes everyone from coders in Cupertino to health aides in Hattiesburg. A growing number of jobs in this huge in-between space—secure and satisfying jobs—can be had by those who earn a credential such as a certificate or industry-recognized certification.

In the future, it's likely there will be no such dichotomy as blue-collar and white-collar jobs. Practical skills matter in all jobs, and so do other human traits such as teamwork, communication, and abstract reasoning. What will matter more is how these abilities are acquired and developed, and how they're synthesized through work into something meaningful.

I don't believe we can or should be satisfied to say the work of the future is what's left over after the machines have their say. There are still lots of jobs that machines could do but don't yet because employing people is less costly than capital investment or companies haven't gotten around to automating their jobs. But these jobs don't have much of a future. People who hold these jobs must always look over their shoulders wondering if theirs will be among the next jobs lost.

We instead should be thinking about the work that won't go away—the work only people can do. It's why I call this kind of work "human work." It is the work upon which our collective future will be based.

What, then, is a more operational definition of human work? For starters, it is work in which the people performing it are actively engaged and responding to their environments. Because the landscape for human work is dynamic, it isn't repetitive and it's much more difficult to automate—good news for us, but less so for the machines. AI gives machines the ability to learn through repetition, but the harder it is to discern patterns, the more likely it is humans will be needed to do it.

The most unpredictable environments are those created by other humans, which is why so much human work involves interacting with people. Human work also involves creativity, including imaginative approaches to solving problems. Another word for this kind of human work is innovation. The ability to come up with new approaches to addressing challenges—no matter how big or small—is of ever-increasing value in most work, if not all.

Ken Goldberg, a noted AI expert, roboticist, and all-around Renaissance guy, thinks a lot about these issues. He's a distinguished artist (with an Emmy nomination to back it up), an inventor (he holds several patents), and the William S. Floyd Jr. Distinguished Chair in Engineering at the University of California, Berkeley. Goldberg has been at the leading edge of the dialogue about what robots, AI, and other smart machines can and cannot do. He told me many commentators at home and abroad have it wrong when they try to understand the capabilities of advanced technologies.

"Humans deal with nuance and subtlety," Goldberg said. "There's no sign that AI is close to understanding these things." He said we should focus instead on the notion of human/machine "complementarity"—the principle "that what humans are good at is complementary to what machines can do, and vice versa."

Goldberg offers what he calls a "radically hopeful" vision for AI and robots, in which society takes advantage of the capabilities of machines, understands their limitations, and refocuses on the human skills and knowledge that define emerging human work.

"We shouldn't be teaching coding to preschoolers," Goldberg observed, reflecting on the proliferation of products and educational strategies that app developers and publishers peddle to teachers. "They need to learn to communicate, collaborate, and build stronger connections to each other as learners." Goldberg said nurturing these foundational human capabilities is key to the lifelong development and continuous growth of human workers.

What all this means is people need to develop the knowledge, skills, and expertise human work requires. Human work is what people need and want, and, by definition, human work calls upon the unique and highly developed talent of individuals for the betterment of society.

The Human Effects of the Transformation of Work

Several years ago, I was talking to a friend about our respective work experiences. I told her how much satisfaction I get out of work, personally and professionally. I find meaning and value in work, I argued. I felt as if my efforts—I was employed as an education policy analyst at the time—were contributing in a small way to something bigger.

She had a different view, saying her job was just a means to an end. Much of her job in health services was repetitive, and she found little joy through work. "Your first clue is that they have to pay you to do it," she argued sarcastically.

This is the dilemma of work in the modern world. While some find meaning and purpose in their work, others see it as strictly transactional: I work, somebody pays. Interestingly, workers in the United States generally agree with my view that there's more to work than just making money. As a recent study from Gallup pointed out, "Enjoying their day-to-day work, having stable and predictable pay, and having a sense of purpose each rate more highly than level of pay among U.S. workers' criteria for job quality—even among those in the bottom 20% of incomes."[22]

But no matter one's view of what work should be, what may be more important is that technology is now changing everything. More tasks that previously required human intervention will be completed through advances in artificial intelligence and automation. Certainly, some jobs may be lost to AI, and others gained. But trying to sort the winners and losers is a fool's errand. There are simply too many variables to know exactly which jobs will be eliminated, or for that matter, which might be created.

We know the expanding capabilities of AI and other digital technologies are leading to new employment structures: empowering workers in some cases and displacing them in others. A new world of human work is emerging, but this does not change the fact that the future of work will include ongoing disruptions of employment on a substantial scale. Yet as we consider these changes, it's easy to lose sight of the massive transformation of the global job market that already has taken place, with profound implications not just for the economy but for the lives of millions of people.

Malaika White is one of those hit hard by this transformation. A single mother of two, a few years ago she suddenly found herself out of work. She had worked fourteen years in a variety of roles for Bank of America before it became clear to her the lack of a college degree limited her opportunities at the bank. She then took a supervisor's job with the government of King County, Washington, but two days before her probation period was to end, the county laid her off. "It was the scariest time of my life," White recalled. "I'd never been out of a job before. It was a point when I was at rock bottom."[23]

That's when she decided she would try again—for the fourth time—to further her education. In the winter of 2015, while in her mid-30s, she enrolled at Seattle Central College. She graduated with an associate degree in the spring of 2018 and is pursuing a bachelor's degree in public affairs at Seattle University.

"I was kind of embarrassed to come back to school," she admitted. "But I always felt I had the potential to do more." This promise went unrealized for decades, even though White had taken a few faltering steps into college before this attempt. Her first try also was at Seattle Central, where she enrolled at age 19. It was there she met the father of her two daughters, DaVonne and Nieela, now teenagers. White acknowledged that back then she "didn't have a clear educational focus." She ended up dropping out after she became pregnant.

During her time at Bank of America, she "always had the desire to get an associate degree." She started and stopped school two more times while she was working at the bank. Those two attempts—one at Seattle Central and the other at a for-profit school that's now out of business—didn't work out, in part, because she couldn't afford child care. This is a challenge many students face: how to live their lives and go to school. "It's often the life circumstances that get in the way of education," said Sheila Edwards Lange, president of Seattle Central. Yoshiko S. Harden, vice president of Seattle Central, said many of the community college's students have "a margin of error that is so narrow. You have your funding, your classes, your car, your apartment. One of those falls, and it's a house of cards."

White's school experience has been different this time because she's taken advantage of the counseling and mentoring Seattle Central has made available to her. Even while enrolled, she had a job in the college's administration office—first working at the front desk and then being promoted several times to more advanced assignments before working for the Seattle Central Foundation. Her fourth time around, everything is working out, she said. "First, there's maturity. I'm much more focused now," she said. "My kids are older. They can take care of themselves. And I'm fortunate to work here, too, and they make my schedule flexible. And my counselors help me every step of the way."

Millions of people have similar stories. While White had a good job in a large, established company, this didn't insulate her from the changes sweeping through her industry—banking—or the overall economy. Although she had been doing well, with a stable job and solid middle-class lifestyle, White found herself out of work and facing an uncertain future. It wasn't just a job and income that had gone away—she had lost her place in the economy, work she was good at, and her ability to provide for her children.

Fortunately for White, and others like her, the story did not end there. As with so many others in today's economy, she found the route back involved investing in herself and developing her knowledge, skills, and abilities. She found her way to and through a community college. For others, the path can be through a bachelor's-granting institution, a competency-based online program, an apprenticeship, company-sponsored education and training, or myriad options for learning what individuals need to know to succeed in a changing world.

Looking back, it's clear the shift away from an industrial-age job market began decades ago as the demand for talent, particularly people with technical skills, increased.[24] As technological change swept through the economy, it affected all jobs in all sectors. Skill demands began increasing as industries and occupations were transformed. This steady progression meant those without more advanced skills were cut off from good jobs and opportunities for advancement. Because this transformation of jobs was not widely recognized or fully understood, employers, policymakers, and education systems were slow to respond.

In the United States, all of this came to a head in 2008. The Great Recession has been described by the U.S. labor economist Anthony Carnevale as "a smart bomb targeting low-skill jobs." It was worse for many workers. Entire industries that had employed large numbers of low-skilled workers were wiped out.

Jobs came back from the depth of the recession, but they were not the same jobs that were lost. From December 2007 to January 2010, the economy shed a net total of 7.4 million jobs, 5.6 million of them for people with a high school education or less. Through early 2020, the economy had added more than 8 million jobs, almost all for people with some college experience or a college degree. Of the 5.6 million jobs lost for people with a high school education or less, only 80,000 ever came back.[25] From the pandemic job loss data, it's clear this cycle from the 2008 recession is beginning to repeat itself.

This same pattern of low-skilled jobs being replaced by ones requiring higher-level skills and credentials beyond a high school diploma is happening throughout the world. OECD's 2018 report on employment used similar language to describe the trends in their more than thirty member countries: "The jobs destroyed during the crisis are not the same as those created in the recovery. Leading firms are in great demand of highly qualified personnel, with high-level cognitive skills—such as complex

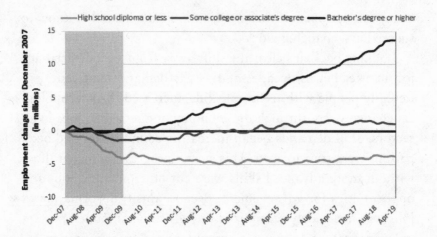

Figure 1. Since the end of the Great Recession, almost all job growth has been in jobs that require advanced learning.
Source: Georgetown University Center on Education and the Workforce, 2019.

problem-solving, critical thinking, and creativity—and social in-telligence—social perceptiveness needed when persuading, nego-tiating, and caring for others. These skills are in short supply in many countries and people who possess them have been the main beneficiaries of wage growth."[26]

However, many workers are not well equipped to meet the rapidly emerging labor-market demand for these higher-level skills. According to OECD's Survey of Adult Skills, almost half of adults in OECD countries have at best only a basic ability to solve problems using technology. This means they have no fa-miliarity with computers at all or only can solve problems "that involve few steps and explicit criteria, such as sorting emails into pre-existing folders."[27]

Drilling down into the data on jobs is even more revealing about how talent has become the arbiter of opportunity. In the United States, the preponderance of good jobs—defined as those that pay at least $35,000 a year and have benefits such as health care and retirement—available to Americans with just a high school diploma has fallen from a third of all jobs in 1991 to just

20% today. Meanwhile, the number of good jobs *is* growing, but they're nearly all going to people with credentials, including degrees, certificates, professional or industry-recognized certifications, or other earned qualifications.

So why are credentials awarded after high school so valuable that Malaika White and people like her want them badly enough to overcome barriers to earn them? It's an important question, and one some people find easy to trivialize. In their view, students are like proverbial sheep, pursuing formal learning in outdated structures and earning degrees they don't need and can't use simply for their prestige value. In sum, these critics say employers' preference for people with credentials beyond a high school diploma is mere "signaling" or a form of "credential creep."[28]

These arguments are, at best, wishful thinking and, at worst, an attempt to hang on to the privilege naysayers who make these arguments believe college degrees often signify. The truth is the demand for these credentials by both students and employers is a response to a real shift that has taken place in the knowledge economy—the shift to a talent-based job market.

As dramatic as the effects of technology and automation have been on jobs and workers, we face a future in which these shifts accelerate. Most observers believe the coming transformation of work caused by rapid advances in artificial intelligence will be even more disruptive, with erratic, sudden, and severe effects on particular occupations and populations.

Anxiety about the effects of AI on jobs is not limited to pundits and futurists—it is widespread and global. According to a poll on people's attitudes toward AI conducted by Northeastern University and Gallup, most people in the United States, Canada, and the United Kingdom, which includes England, Scotland, Wales, and Northern Ireland, claim they have solid understandings of AI. Fifty-five percent in the United States, 54% in Canada, and 52% in the United Kingdom say so, with younger people, not surprisingly, being more likely to say they understand it. But this supposed understanding does not foster confidence. Most people in all three countries believe AI's effects will be negative. More than 60% of adults in Canada and the United Kingdom believe AI will eliminate more jobs than it creates, and more than 70% of Americans agree.[29]

The source of the widespread belief that AI will have adverse effects is obvious. After all, over the course of decades, technology has altered many if not most jobs. But until now, job loss because of technology, while significant, mostly has been limited to jobs based on repetitive or highly specific tasks, whether in lower-wage fields such as construction and manufacturing, or in higher-wage fields such as accounting and law.

The remaining jobs in high-wage occupations in which repetitive tasks are important could be hit hard by the spread of AI. Accounting giant Deloitte reported almost 40% of jobs in the legal sector could be automated within the next two decades.[30] And research based on data from Oxford University in 2016 predicted up to 95% of jobs in the accounting sector could be eliminated over time.[31]

This asymmetry in job losses will continue to evolve and change over time. But it likely will be concentrated in specific occupations and industries and will hit regions where these occupations and industries predominate. And make no mistake—coming advances in technology and artificial intelligence will lead to the elimination of more jobs. An oft-cited analysis by McKinsey lays out the sobering statistics.[32] By 2030, 375 million people worldwide are likely to need to change occupations. On a percentage basis, the effects are greatest in the most advanced economies—a third of workers in the United States and Germany, and half of workers in Japan, could be displaced.

Again, whether the job losses caused by AI are widespread or are more focused isn't the headline. More important is that available data suggest people are not ready for changes in work on the horizon. While large majorities believe AI will eliminate jobs in the future, only 37% of workers in Canada and 34% in the United Kingdom worry their own jobs are threatened by technology or artificial intelligence. And, get this—only 17% of workers in the United States are fearful about their jobs on this front.[33] People shouldn't panic, but frankly, this looks like complacency.

The Structure of Work Is Changing, Too

Work is being transformed by more than the evolution of jobs as AI takes over the more repetitive tasks people used to do. We are also seeing a strong shift away from long-term employment to shorter-term work. A big part of this is explained by the emergence of new, short-term employment structures—the so-called "gig economy." The rise of companies such as Uber, TaskRabbit, and Airbnb has been well documented. But this emergence of on-demand solutions to help make people's lives easier is just the beginning.

More broadly, we are seeing a large increase in the proportion of workers for whom contract work, digital marketplaces, and other short-term, contingent arrangements are replacing full-time employment and careers. According to McKinsey, about a quarter of people working in the United States and Europe are classified as "independent workers."[34] The OECD reported in 2019 that one of every nine workers in the world's most advanced nations is working on a temporary contract—in effect, short-term "jobs" without long-term prospects.[35] Both sources note the number of these workers is expected to grow as digital marketplaces become more widespread and displaced workers use independent contractor or temporary work to re-enter the workforce.

Attitudes toward changes in careers and work were probed by the Pearson Global Learner Survey, conducted by the Harris Poll. As the name implies, the survey draws on data from nineteen countries to provide a unique global perspective on how changes in work and careers are being experienced. The authors describe the shifts in attitudes as the emergence of a "reinvention mindset among workers. Globally, 70% of people agree working for a single employer for their entire career is "old-fashioned," and 84% agree with the statement "my career path will be significantly different from my parents' or grandparents'."[36]

In one sense, concerns about these shifts in the workforce are nothing new. In the late 1980s in the United States, under President Ronald Reagan, a massive effort was undertaken to study issues of workforce quality and labor market efficiency. A blue-ribbon commission, led by prominent voices from the business, labor, and education fields, was formed to look at the long-term issues of work and workers in an increasingly technology-driven labor market. The commission contracted with dozens of analysts and researchers—me included—to explore "increasing the excellence of the American workforce." Several papers took direct aim at the issue of independent workers and temporary employment. Rebecca Blank, for example, the former Princeton University economist and current University of Wisconsin-Madison chancellor, observed this phenomenon "is a significant aspect of the U.S. labor market, and has been increasing in importance over the past decades."[37]

While it is certainly not new, the label we overuse to describe this trend—"gig economy,"—is an international phenomenon. The platforms that support such work are, by their nature, scalable across political boundaries. Even as we have grown somewhat accustomed to the pace of change in today's economy, it is remarkable to realize Uber launched its ride-sharing service in April 2012 and now operates in at least sixty-five countries.

It's not at all clear governments can do much to change the trajectory of these contingent work platforms, even if they wanted to. After a recent trip to Costa Rica, a friend reported he was happy to see the Uber app on his phone working fine, with many cars available. But he was amused when the drivers asked him to sit up front—leaving his wife in the back—to make it less likely they'd be stopped by police. If they were stopped, they were asked to say the driver was an old friend who had stopped by to give them a lift. It turns out that despite the fully functioning app, ready supply of cars, and enthusiastic drivers, Uber was not legal in Costa Rica at that time.

While making deliveries and driving for Uber may not be a high-skill occupation, the "uberization" of work is spreading to occupations in which people's skills are the decisive factor. In fact, leading thinkers such as Roger Martin, a management expert and former business school dean at the University of Toronto, are referring to the emergence of a "talent economy."[38] In the talent economy, highly skilled workers operate as independent contractors in order to maximize their opportunities and incomes.[39] Unlike the "Uber economy"—providing ready access to undifferentiated workers and services at low cost—the major driver of the talent economy is quality, not cost. People with knowledge and skills in demand are finding these shifts an attractive alternative to customary employment practices. While they only make up 20% of the contingent workforce, people making more than $100,000 per year are its fastest-growing segment.[40]

But whether working as a part-time Uber driver or an in-demand IT professional, people in contingent work arrangements face a new set of problems, from access to health care and retirement to assuring long-term security and social relationships. Today, it seems impossible to overstate the effects this transformation of the job market has had on people worldwide. For some—those with the requisite knowledge, skills, and abilities—the talent economy is increasing opportunity, allowing better life-work balance, and creating a greater sense of well-being. For others, the uncertainty around work is a growing problem with potentially devastating effects for individuals and society.

Good Jobs, Human Work, and the Quality of Life

Holding a good job, or at least being able to find good work, has become inextricably linked to well-being and the quality of life. The talent economy creates many opportunities for those with the necessary knowledge, skills, and abilities. For those without in-demand talent, it is ruthless. The consequences of being left out of the economy are no longer abstract—they are directly measured in life expectancy and other social indicators. The United States is now going backward on many of these indicators, and the failure to nurture and develop talent appears to be the culprit.

A groundbreaking 2015 research paper[41] by Anne Case and Angus Deaton and their 2017 follow-up[42] revealed exactly what is at stake in the growing relationship between talent and quality of life. Their analysis of mortality data, broken down by race and level of education, shows a truly disturbing rise in "deaths of despair" among white working-class people, especially those who are high school dropouts or have never obtained recognized learning after high school. What seems to be happening is these millions of Americans are losing faith in the possibility of economic opportunity and social mobility—that is, the foundation of the American Dream. These trends will only get worse unless we can nurture and develop the talent of all people.

Since Case and Deaton first raised the specter that rising mortality rates among middle-aged, working-class whites represent deaths of despair, other researchers have looked into the data to better understand the rising inequity and unfairness of increased mortality—the fact that Americans die at significantly different rates based on economic status, education levels, and other factors.

While Case and Deaton focused on working-class whites, it has long been known mortality rates for African Americans are significantly higher across the board than those for whites. Researchers have found that among African American and older whites not included in the Case and Deaton analysis, premature deaths caused by cardiovascular disease and cancers explain most of the difference rather than the three causes labeled deaths of despair—suicide, alcoholic liver disease, and drug overdose. This is hardly comforting, however. According to the researchers, the data show the long-term psychological and physiological effects of coping with stress resulting from their precarious and worsening economic and social situations is a major factor in the higher mortality rates among these Americans.[43]

Much evidence supports the idea that fears of a decline in economic opportunity are well grounded. A study released in 2019 reveals the shocking extent of accelerating wealth inequality in America.[44] Out of the total assets of $114 trillion owned by Americans in 2018, the wealthiest 10% owned 70% of the total, up from 61% in 1989. Meanwhile, the bottom 50% of American households had virtually no net worth at all—down from 4% of the total in 1989 to 1% in 2018.

Sadly, this has long been the reality for millions of nonwhite Americans. In 1989, median white household wealth totaled $424,000, compared with just $78,000 for African American families and $84,000 for Latino households. By 2016, white wealth had grown to an average of $919,000, compared with $139,000 for African American families and $172,000 for Latino families. While income inequality has received heightened attention in recent years—and deservedly so—it's clear wealth inequality is an even greater problem. *continue WORK = wealth ?*

Of course, both disparities reflect a third problem, which is the stark divide across racial and ethnic groups in educational outcomes after high school and the earning opportunities that provides. In 2018, 48% of whites had completed associate or bachelor's degrees, compared with just 32% of African Americans and 25% of Latinos.

Also, geography is an underreported factor that compounds the steep challenges facing the United States's poor households and people of color. Residents living along the southern border with Mexico, for example, many of whom are Latino immigrants, face an array of discriminatory education and workforce training practices.

While portraits of displaced manufacturing workers in Rust Belt states or coal miners in the Appalachian region—many of them white—were common after the 2008 recession began, less prominent were the stories of those for whom persistent discrimination stretches back generations. In the Black Rural South, an area comprising 157 counties where African Americans are more than 35% of the population, significant injustice exists. More than 60% of African Americans in the rural South have a high school diploma or less, while only 10% of African Americans in the region have a bachelor's degree. African Americans are overrepresented among those with low educational attainment compared to all other racial and ethnic groups.

The exclusion of these communities from the dialogue about preparing and deploying future workers is not only unjust, it is also unwise. As a report from the Joint Center for Political and Economic Studies notes:

> Any future of work discussion that excludes the Black Rural South is incomplete. We cannot build a modern system that fully transitions American workers to a new economy without consciously addressing the past, present, and future of the Black Rural South. Continued neglect of the residents of the Black Rural South sets the stage to neglect the residents of other regions with industries of declining significance—such as the Industrial Midwest, Appalachia, and eventually Silicon Valley.[45]

All this shows how work is central to our lives and the health of communities and nations. For many, work is still just a job, but even so, not all jobs are created equal. The divide between good jobs and not-so-good jobs is increasingly stark and important to the overall quality of life of people and communities. But what is a good job? Economists have come up with different criteria, but most include pay above poverty level and access to health care and retirement as decisive factors.[46]

Perhaps we can learn more about what makes a job good by asking workers themselves. Gallup's Great Jobs Survey does that, and it found workers consider factors beyond pay and benefits as necessary for jobs to be considered good. Workers value job security and predictability along with higher wages, and they

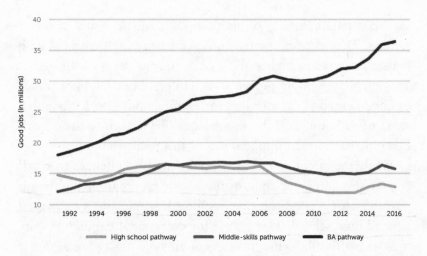

Figure 2. Good jobs (those that pay at least $35,000 for workers 25–44 and at least $45,000 for workers 45–64) are going to people with more advanced learning.
Source: Georgetown University Center on Education and the Workforce analysis of data from the U.S. Census Bureau and Bureau of Labor Statistics, *Current Population Survey*, 1992–2017.

also consider factors such as career advancement opportunities and having a sense of purpose and dignity important as well.[47] About 40% of Americans consider their jobs to be good based on criteria important to them, while 16% say they are in bad jobs. A plurality of Americans (44%) consider their jobs to be mediocre because they lack some characteristics these workers consider important. This might not matter so much were there not ample evidence job satisfaction has a direct bearing on many measures of quality of life.

The likelihood people hold good jobs rather than mediocre or bad ones goes up dramatically with higher levels of education, just as income is higher in jobs that require college-level skills. There is, however, an intriguing exception to this rule. Workers with high school education and professional certifications but no education beyond this are among the most likely to say they are in good jobs: 49% of workers fitting this description have good jobs, compared to 40% of high school graduates without certifications. They even do better on this measure than workers with master's degrees or higher: 47% of them consider their jobs good. This surprising finding reveals something about the importance of documented skills, not just for earnings but also for people's sense of the value and the significance they attach to their work. I'll come back to the implications of this reality later.

While the talent economy presents many challenges to workers, we shouldn't lose sight of the simple fact that having the opportunity for a good job now requires learning and a credential beyond high school. This is true for everyone. Real opportunity must exist for all, so in a talent economy we must seek to understand and eliminate racial disparities in educational outcomes after high school wherever we find them. Disparities in educational attainment based on income, geography, age, and especially race aren't acceptable because the consequences of failing to find success in our education system are so severe. As important as it is to increase the proportion of adults with education or training after high school, we should never forget it is a means to an end, and this end is greater economic opportunity and social mobility for all.

The transformation of work is about much more than the economy. It is fundamentally an issue about human flourishing—of prosperity in an era when such success seems increasingly elusive to those without the requisite knowledge, skills, and abilities and the credentials that signify their achievements. Those without quality post–high school credentials are increasingly relegated to dead-end jobs or no jobs at all.

Of course, the knowledge there are large numbers of people without the skills necessary to thrive in this new economy is not new. But many more people are at high risk of joining them through no fault of their own as their jobs are transformed or disappear in unpredictable ways. For many, a world without opportunities for meaningful work is a world of despair.

When it comes to adapting to the transformation of work caused by AI, the data don't paint a rosy picture. Fewer than half of workers say they know what skills will be needed in the future to adapt to the spread of AI (45% in the United States and Canada; 41% in the United Kingdom), and a slightly smaller percentage say they know where they can get the education and training they will need. However, too few people understand the urgency. While almost all workers see value in learning throughout their careers—95% in the United States, 94% in Canada, and 92% in the United Kingdom—few seem to see it as an absolute necessity. Thirty percent of workers in Canada and the United Kingdom believe their skills will never become obsolete or dated, while 42% of workers in the United States believe this, and an additional 22% say it will be ten years or more before their skills lose relevance. (I'm assuming a lot of these people say they'll be comfortably retired by then).[48]

This is frankly a ticking time bomb—both for them and for the economy. The scale of the shifts affecting work is at least of the same magnitude as the Industrial Revolution.[49] That's a dangerous reality. While social and economic support structures eventually were transformed worldwide by the Industrial Revolution, we should pause to consider the resulting disruptions and how long it took to overcome them. Chief among them was the need to dramatically increase education levels across the entire population as vast numbers of people abandoned rural areas for jobs in factories and new lives in cities. Eventually, the Industrial Revolution prompted the introduction of universal primary and secondary education throughout the world—a massive accomplishment for the common good.

The technological revolution requires a response at a similar scale, including a similarly dramatic increase in education levels across the board. Indeed, the time has come to commit to universal learning beyond high school—assuring everyone can gain the knowledge, skills, and abilities needed to thrive in a changing economy and world throughout life.

Human Work, Fairness, and Opportunity

The new knowledge economy creates many opportunities for those with talent, but for those with talent deficits, it is ruthless and unfair. Those who have not developed their knowledge and skills, as represented by a college degree or other credential after high school, are increasingly relegated to lives of hardship and struggle. In this labor market, economic opportunity and social mobility require effective learning throughout life. As mentioned earlier, the consequences of not getting this learning already are devastating for individuals and families and are no longer abstract. They can be directly measured in life expectancy and other key social indicators. In the future, the effects will only increase.

More people are falling below the threshold at which economic opportunity and social mobility are possible, and as more drop off, social stresses can lead to seismic fissures in democratic nations. In the United States, people are segregated not only by race, geography, and income but also by education levels. The rising tide of human learning needs will submerge more and more people if our education systems and the labor market do not adapt soon to these demands—and with devastating societal consequences. People need to reskill and up-skill more frequently in today's economy. And expanding opportunity for learning after high school is an essential response to the challenges arising from the shifting nature of work.

In education, there has been a decades-old debate about the quality of the learning experience compared with the opportunity it creates by race, income, and other factors. Yet we now know this is really a false dichotomy. Quality learning without equitable outcomes—in other words, fairness—is merely the reproduction of privilege. More people of color with credentials of low quality is a broken promise, a systemic failure that exacerbates the unfairness they and others face.[50]

The implications of this shift in the learning enterprise—whether formal learning in colleges and universities, workforce training programs, or the acquisition of knowledge and skills in less formal contexts—are profound. This shift is also affecting job markets and the way work is organized and structured. We must recognize that talent already has emerged as the primary arbiter of employment. This demand in the job market for talent puts *people*—diverse groups of learners and workers—at the center of the new human work ecosystem.

But the dominant narrative about the effects of technology on jobs hasn't been about talent—it's been about winners and losers. We talk about how some people, especially those with technical skills, are thriving while others are left behind with declining standards of living. Mass media tends to accentuate this winners-vs.-losers storyline. Numerous stories have focused on how some technology companies such as Apple, Facebook, and Twitter have become fabulously profitable while some of the oldest and most established brands, including Sears and Kodak, have become irrelevant or disappeared entirely. Meanwhile, we read that the regions where tech companies are located are dynamic and growing while other, less fortunate areas are mired in downward spirals of decay and depression. The bottom line of this winners-and-losers narrative is some people will move ahead to bright futures while others will be doomed.

Given the prevalence of this narrative, it is not surprising some people see themselves as victims of an unfair system and uncaring "elites," while others unfairly see their good fortune as evidence of better personal decisions or even innate superiority. As the effects of AI move through the economy and affect all sectors and occupations, we can only hope this narrative of winners and losers will die out.

Yet we don't know what kind of narrative will replace it. It could be an even more defeatist one of "there are not enough jobs so we might as well pay people not to work." Or it could be a dystopian storyline about how technology is our true enemy and a threat to life itself. But I shudder to consider the consequences of framing our social and economic debates in these terms. If we take the right steps, a more hopeful narrative can emerge—one based on the idea that technology allows us to focus on what it means to be human and to do human work.

To construct this narrative, though, we need to understand more about what human work is and how it will affect the economy and society. Seeing human work through the eyes of the workers themselves is one way to begin.

The Work Only Humans Can Do

I work all day at the factory,
I'm building a machine that's not for me,
There must be a reason that I can't see,
You've got to humanize yourself.
          —The Police, "Rehumanize Yourself," 1981

Human work is on full display at a San Francisco–based organization called Safe & Sound, which works "to prevent child abuse and reduce its devastating impact." CEO Katie Albright, a former deputy city attorney and leading child advocate and education expert, personally exemplifies many of the qualities that define the human worker model.

Talking with her in 2019 at the organization's headquarters in an old Victorian fire station, I was struck by how her language about the people served by Safe & Sound, and the staff members who work with those clients, represents the vanguard of this human work paradigm. Albright is deeply compassionate toward the people she works with. She is rooted in the idea that critically judging and evaluating what works and what doesn't is key to the organization's success. She has a strong ethical focus that drives her work. And she uses her powerful communication skills, which often involve "actively listening," to constantly adapt the techniques used to address the root causes of child abuse.

"So much of what we do centers on establishing or rebuilding trust," Albright said as we toured the facility. "Our task is to empower people to understand and address their own trauma, keep children safe, and help build stronger community." By community, Albright means both literally in the city and region, but also among the individuals participating in the organization's services. Safe & Sound's team of sixty employees and about one hundred volunteers serves an active family cohort of 1,200 at any given time, and works with more than 12,000 people annually through a wide array of services including counseling, trust-building exercises, and basic needs provision (such as meals) both in person and by telephone.

Albright said the task of preparing herself and the team for the work of addressing family needs to prevent child abuse never ends. Staff members are constantly being trained, supported, and reskilled to keep up with the latest research, field-based knowledge, and counseling techniques. "They are doing human work, and that means they can never stop learning," she said. "And so are the parents we serve. Teaching them how to be better parents has a real impact on the safety and happiness of their families."

Albright shared a manual used to train staff and volunteers who work on their twenty-four-hour parental stress phone support line. The manual, more than sixty pages long, is replete with illustrations and examples of how team members need to develop and hone their active listening techniques, mindfulness, and other key traits. It's a constantly evolving process of development and training, according to Albright, as research and experience continue to guide the important, lifesaving work Safe & Sound does.

So, let's return to the question. What *is* human work? Katie Albright and her colleagues at Safe & Sound point in the direction of an answer: human work is the work only humans can do. It blends our human traits, such as compassion, empathy, ethics, and personal communication, with our developed human capabilities, such as critical analysis, judgment of quality, and anticipation of what others might do. It requires knowledge and skill.

And human work brings together the things that give us meaning and allow us to continue to flourish over time, including learning, earning money, and serving others.

Make no mistake, being paid for work—having a job, making a living—matters. Everyone needs an income to survive, but for most people, paid work represents something more. It's an expression of position in the world, identity, and sense of self-worth. And paid work and the jobs people hold are changing dramatically, even if they aren't going away. But human work is not merely about a job. It is about meaning and opportunity; it is what we *do as humans*. It is core to our existence. Work is aspirational. The phrase "my work is never done" is, in reality, a good thing. A job is a component of human work, but the two are not synonymous.

This is a case where a learning task most of us acquired early in life—consulting a dictionary—can help. According to the *Oxford English Dictionary*, work is an "activity involving mental or physical effort done in order to achieve a purpose or result," while a job is simply "a paid position of regular employment." Certainly, people work while on the job, at least some of the time, but not all work is a job. I find it interesting effort alone is not enough to qualify an activity as work. The essential quality of human work is it serves a purpose or leads to a result.

Of course, some work is paid when the purpose or result is of financial value to someone else. But even then, work has meaning to the person who performs it. This meaning may come from the satisfaction of having and applying expertise. It can come from a sense of doing something of use to the greater society, or the pride of providing for people important to us. But whatever the purpose, work has meaning whether it is a paid job or not. Work is core to our existence, and when the ability to perform meaningful work is taken away, it is devastating to people and societies.

Service to others is another kind of work that brings meaning to our lives. No matter how large or small the effort, to serve others is a key to a satisfying and rewarding life. Service is also essential to building healthy communities and a stronger society. Like all work, service requires effort toward some purpose, and it also draws on people's knowledge and skills in the way jobs do. Of course, many use money gained through work to be of service to others, as well as support themselves.

Work is no longer just about jobs—if it ever was. Earning, learning, and serving is the new paradigm. Developing one's abilities throughout life and applying them to make a living and improve the lives of others are the three core activities everyone must have the opportunity to do. Without all three, the quality of our lives suffers. Just as at Safe & Sound, human work blends learning, earning, and serving, because together these things articulate our shared or collective obligations both to one another and ourselves.

The New Occupations of Human Work

How many times do people ask, "What do you do for a living?" Whether it's an innocuous conversation starter or the first question border control agents ask of people who arrive on international flights, the question has always caught me by surprise. We're accustomed to answering the question with a simple, one-word answer: attorney, accountant, machinist, farmer, teacher, or any of many other possibilities. In fact, the U.S. Bureau of Labor Statistics classifies every worker in America as belonging to one of 867 distinct occupations. If, like me, you've never had an occupation that fits neatly into one of those categories, you may have an inkling of what the future holds for millions of workers.

Human work doesn't fit into the neat categories of the industrial age. Rather than mastering a single body of knowledge or set of technical skills, to do human work, people must develop a wide range of abilities and apply them to solving complex problems in dynamic settings. As we saw from examining the effects of technology on jobs, if a job can be defined by a single body of knowledge, no matter how arcane, or a single set of skills, no matter how specialized, there is a high likelihood artificial intelligence can do it.

What data and research are pointing toward is the emergence of new kinds of occupations—or shifts in existing ones that make them scarcely recognizable and demand entirely new sets of skills. Four kinds of occupations are emerging that embody human work—the work of the future.

1. *Helpers.*

These are people in occupations involving deep personal interaction with other people. In today's service economy, these jobs are everywhere, as many industries have transformed to become focused on customers.

This can be clearly seen in financial services. As technology has taken over most of the repetitive tasks professionals such as bankers and accountants used to do, their jobs have become focused on understanding client needs and responding to them. As retail banking has become the key driver of profits in that industry, recognition of the importance of customer service has become widespread. One survey found the top investment priority of banking executives in most of the world (Europe, Asia-Pacific, and emerging markets) was to enhance customer service, with implementing new technology far behind.[1] The survey also reported that bank executives view talent as the primary constraint they face in pursuing their customer-centric business model.

A growing number of helping professions can be found in health care, with the fastest-growing occupations including recreational and occupational therapists, nutritionists and dietitians, and mental health care providers. European studies have shown patient-centered models improve health outcomes: "When patients are genuinely involved in health care decisions and their preferences are listened to and acted on, the result is better health, more engaged patients and lower costs."[2]

One of the most exciting aspects of helping professions is they can offer a route to advancement for many people who have been left behind in the economy. The story of Jaquan Gordon taught me a lot about this. As with millions of kids before him, Gordon got a high school job working in a grocery store. But Gordon was fortunate enough to get a job at Wegmans in Perinton, New York, about fifteen miles southeast of Rochester. Wegmans put him into a program designed to develop the abilities of young people to provide excellent customer service, a key differentiator and competitive advantage in the supermarket industry. The lessons began simply—always look the customer straight in the eye and offer a strong handshake—but they didn't end there.[3]

Wegmans offered Gordon the chance to learn while he worked to become a customer service representative in one of its supermarkets. While dealing with shoppers' complaints and handling refunds may not sound glamorous, it's a high-profile position at Wegmans and one the company considers to be on the management track. Gordon is now the first in his family to pursue higher education—he's majoring in business administration while working at Wegmans. "Before I started this program, I was just another black kid on the street with no job," he said. "First time I walked through that door, I knew this is where I wanted to be, and that I was going to challenge myself to be better."

2. Bridgers.

People in these occupations interact with others, perform technical tasks, and help run systems. Bridgers literally create connections—to other people, and to other forms of work. Sales managers, automotive repair managers, and many supervisors fall into this category. So, too, do jobs in information technology. The notion of IT professionals as introverted "computer geeks" is long gone. Today, IT professionals must be Bridgers, combining technical expertise with strong people skills such as communication and empathy to be effective. This is the killer combination that makes Bridgers indispensable to the organizations that employ them.

Rodney Owens has made the transition to human work by combining technical and people skills. Owens had spent nearly a quarter century building a business customizing cars and motor-cycles in Charlotte, North Carolina, before a falling-out with a business partner forced him to reassess his life and career. "When all of the fun got sucked out of my career, I sat down and realized I wasn't happy with my life. Even with the success in business, it felt like there was something missing."

Over the years, Owens had taken courses to learn to use the ever-changing machinery in his business, but in 2013, at age 40, he decided to pursue a degree at Central Piedmont Community College in Charlotte. He admits he was not a good student in high school, but he was determined to apply himself upon resuming his education. He sped through his program and earned an associate degree in computer-integrated machining. He finished with a perfect 4.0 grade point average.

During his time as a student, Owens and others at Central Piedmont realized he worked well with his fellow students. So Central Piedmont asked him to teach. "Early on, it was apparent Rodney had a gift for being able to relate to his classmates," said Eric Easton, senior program coordinator in Central Piedmont's engineering division. "They viewed him as a role model they could look up to and go to for guidance."

Owens is a Bridger. He draws on his technical expertise in computer-aided machining and his real-world experience building and running a business to guide his students to achieve their own goals. His work with students extends beyond Central Piedmont classrooms. He counsels students about the opportunities they will have after high school, and he does private tutoring in local high schools, reminding students "there are other opportunities if they don't want to go immediately to a four-year college." His influence has even rubbed off on his own family—one of Owens's two daughters has decided to follow his path to Central Piedmont, and his son plans to spend two years at the community college before going on to pursue a bachelor's degree.

Owens offers his students another important lesson. As Easton puts it, Owens provides "an example to all students that at any stage of life, you can return to school and achieve anything you put your mind to. Rodney is living proof that it's never too late to continue one's education."

3. Integrators.

These people are in occupations that integrate knowledge and skills from a range of fields and apply them in a highly personal way. Social workers and elementary school teachers are prime examples.

Social workers must not only keep abreast of knowledge in fields as diverse as psychology, economics, and nutrition, they must also understand the implications of emerging research and be able to integrate it into their practices. Indeed, they are researchers themselves—testing new approaches, innovating, and constantly seeking new ways to better meet the needs of their clients. All this is done within a social, cultural, and economic context, and under constraints of laws and regulations that also are constantly changing.

Integrators also can be people who apply the lessons learned in one context, perhaps over the course of many years, to new or different fields. Paul Helmke embodies this practice. Fifty years after he began a career in public life as student body president at Indiana University, he is back at the university teaching a new generation of students the lessons he's learned as an elected official, lawyer, and issues advocate.

As a professor of practice at Indiana's Paul H. O'Neill School of Public and Environmental Affairs, Helmke is the founding director of the school's Civic Leaders Living-Learning Center. Started in 2013, the center now has one hundred first-year students who live together on three floors of an IU dormitory and study together in regular classes and attend lectures by guests Helmke has known during his career.

Helmke graduated from IU in 1970 and attended law school at Yale University, where he met other aspiring public servants such as Bill Clinton and Hillary Rodham. He practiced law for several years and ran unsuccessfully for a U.S. House seat before he was elected in 1987 to the first of three terms as mayor of Fort Wayne, a northeast Indiana city with 270,989 residents in 2020. He served as president of the U.S. Conference of Mayors during his final term in office. In 1998, Helmke was the Republican nominee for the U.S. Senate in Indiana, losing the race to a former Democratic governor, Evan Bayh. Helmke also lost a primary for a U.S. House seat in 2002.

In 2006, Helmke became president of the Brady Campaign to Prevent Gun Violence, a group founded by Sarah and James Brady, President Ronald Reagan's press secretary who was wounded in an assassination attempt on the president in 1981. Helmke stayed in this high-profile job for five years, becoming one of the gun-control lobby's most quoted spokespeople.

"During my whole career—as a lawyer, helping people with the legal system, as a mayor, getting neighborhood groups involved, and at the Brady Campaign, engaging people on an important issue—my main interest has been, 'How do you get people engaged in government and public affairs?' That's what really appealed to me about doing this," he said.

In class, "I talk about my past experiences, and that's fun: stories from my career as mayor, stories from the Brady days. I try to tie it all in," he said.

Helmke's students come from many backgrounds and interests. About two-thirds are majors in public and environmental affairs, but he also helps select students with other majors. "I want them to know how to talk to people who are doing something different than they are," Helmke said. He lectures on topics including communications law, law and public affairs, urban problems and solutions, legal history and public policy, and democratic institutions and ideals in classical and contemporary Greece.

He also regularly brings in guest lecturers such as former Indiana congressman Lee H. Hamilton, photojournalist Andrea Bruce, and former IU athletic director Fred Glass. Helmke said Glass's story—he started as an intern in politics, rising to become Governor Bayh's chief of staff, later getting involved in attracting a Super Bowl to Indianapolis and then becoming athletic director at a Big Ten university—teaches a lesson he emphasizes often with his students.

"There can be a lot of chance and randomness in your career," he said. "You have to be flexible and adjust. There are various ways you can be successful and have an impact, but you have to learn to switch careers and do different things. You have to be active, network, meet new people, and be ready to take advantage of opportunities."

All students in Helmke's program are required to do philanthropic projects each semester "to push them to do something outside their comfort zone," he said. Students have also started their own advocacy groups to promote sensible gun regulation and increase opportunities for women in politics.

Graduates of the program have gone on to law school, graduate schools, staff jobs on Capitol Hill, and even the comedy scene in Chicago. Each year, IU honors outstanding seniors, and in recent years, Helmke's students have been among those recognized. And in 2019, one of his students became IU's student body president, fifty years after Helmke held the same office.

"I spent my life trying to make a difference," he said. "Here, if I can get ten to twenty kids each year who are going to go out there and make a difference, that's very rewarding. It makes me optimistic about the future."

I believe another aspect to the role of Integrators is extremely important but has tended to go unnoticed until recently: the role of storyteller and the importance of narratives in almost all aspects of our society. The Nobel Prize–winning economist Robert Shiller writes about the importance of narratives in his field and how storytelling doesn't just interpret or explain economic events but likely plays a crucial role in shaping them.[4] The same is true in all other fields and in settings large and small. After all, storytelling is intrinsic to our humanity and is often how we make sense of and find meaning in the world. As Jean-Paul Sartre observed in his 1938 novel, *Nausea*, "A man is always a teller of tales, he lives surrounded by his stories and the stories of others, he sees everything that happens to him through them; and he tries to live his life as if he were recounting it."

4. Creators.

The people in these occupations possess highly technical skills and pure creativity. These might be the people your mother told you were "the creative types."

Many of these occupations involve the creative use of technology. Computer gaming is now a $135 billion global industry, and it is growing at the rate of 11% per year.[5] The sales of one game—*Red Dead Redemption II*—totaled $725 million in its first three days on the market. Video game development employs more than 220,000 people in the United States, at an average salary of $97,000 per year.[6]

Consider Mark Sciarra, who really knows how to improvise. He's been doing it for more than forty years, finding novel ways to stay employed in what he calls "a vicious, cutthroat business" that has undergone major changes. He's not a video game developer, but he applies highly technical skills and a lot of creativity to a different branch of the entertainment industry. Now in his 60s, "with two fake hips and more bumps than I can count," he's still working in his chosen field: professional wrestling. But now he's teaching a new generation how to follow in his footsteps. "I guess you could say you've got to evolve," Sciarra said.

Better known to fans of late-night televised wrestling shows as Rip Rogers or simply as The Hustler, Sciarra has been working steadily in wrestling since 1977, when he bolted from his first job out of college, teaching at an Indiana high school, to take a wrestling gig during a holiday weekend. He never looked back. He performed regularly, sometimes doing more than 300 shows a year, from 1977 to 2000. He worked all over the United States, as well as in Canada and overseas, in Austria, Germany, Great Britain, and South Africa.

Often playing the bad guy in the in-the-ring dramas, Rip Rogers gained a reputation for his antics when he lost a match: madly racing around the ring, claiming his opponent had cheated by pulling his hair or winning on a short count for a pin. With long bleached-blond hair and a black beard, he also burnished his image among wrestling fans as a member of several tag teams with names such as Convertible Blondes, Fabulous Freebirds, Hollywood Blonds, and Midnight Cowboys.

He learned to adapt and change, depending on his surroundings. "When you would go into different places, you would reinvent yourself," he said. "You might shave your hair, or cut your beard, or change your act. A lot of it was nothing original. Everything I did I had seen someplace else maybe forty years ago, but the people in that audience hadn't seen it."

The business changed greatly during his career, Sciarra lamented. When he started, professional wrestling was largely divided into regional territorial businesses. One group, for example, would produce and market all the shows in one state or a multistate region. This dominant group would also have its own local and regional television deals. Wrestlers might bounce from region to region every few years, as Sciarra often did. But in those days, there was plenty of work to go around, with about 800 wrestlers working full-time, many doing shows every night of the week.

In those days, a novice learned the business during late-night van rides from one gig to the next. The older wrestlers would both haze and instruct the younger ones, Sciarra said. The older wrestlers typically played the bad guys in the ring because the bad guys control more of the action and thus can protect both men in the ring from injury, Sciarra observed.

It was still a tough business, he said. Established stars didn't always welcome new talent, fearing a challenge to their good jobs. Injuries could put people out of work, and Sciarra said when he saw another bleached-blond wrestler show up, "you knew they were going to get rid of you." But with the advent of national cable television, the old regional territorial system largely dissolved, and the business became dominated by large corporations such as WWE. As a result, there were fewer jobs.

However, at the end of his active career in the ring, Sciarra saw opportunity in the changing landscape. As the old ways of teaching ended, new ways were needed to prepare aspiring wrestlers for the professional circuit. He went to work as the head trainer for Ohio Valley Wrestling in Louisville, Kentucky. Over the years, he's taught scores of wrestlers, many of whom have advanced to the big-time and others who scrape together a living wrestling in smaller shows in out-of-the-way places.

"In my 20s, I was wrestling guys in their 40s, and they would teach you so they wouldn't get hurt," Sciarra said. "Now there's no feeder system, so you've got goofballs wrestling goofballs a lot of the time." Sciarra tries to turn the goofballs into professionals. His course syllabus ranges from training techniques to memorable wrestling moves to marketing advice. In 2018, he was the subject of a book, *The Book on Pro Wrestling: Lessons from Rip Rogers*, by Caleb Hall.

And he has some side gigs, doing podcasts on wrestling, posting videos on YouTube, and performing the occasional stand-up comedy routine. Earlier in his career, he moonlighted by playing briefly on the Washington Generals basketball team, the touring opponents of the Harlem Globetrotters, and he appeared in the "Human Wheels" music video for a high school friend, John Mellencamp. A craft beer, The Hustler, is named after him, complete with an image of him on the label in pink wrestling trunks, bleached-blond hair, and a black beard.

"I didn't get into this business for the money. It was the adventure," he said. "I went back to my high school reunion, and there were guys who were doctors and lawyers, but everybody wanted to hear my stories."

He also remembers a poignant moment just before his father died. Married at 18, his father "had a bunch of kids and two to three jobs. He looked at me and said, 'Mark, you lived.'"

I believe Sciarra's story says more about the future of human work than the numerous examples of jobs eliminated by robots or AI taking over tasks done by people. While technical skills—and hard work—are necessary in his industry, the essential skills of professional wrestlers are creativity and an understanding of human psychology. As his industry changed dramatically around him, Sciarra's is a story of continuous adaptation through learning, and offers lessons we should all heed.

The People-Centered Economy

It's not just occupations that are changing. The way work is organized is also changing at a dizzying pace. New ways of organizing work are emerging rapidly—freelance work through internet platforms, new kinds of entrepreneurship, and team-based projects in which talent across a range of fields works together to devise solutions to problems. This is the shift away from traditional jobs mentioned earlier, and it's happening much more rapidly and to many more people than we realize.

One such person is John Hlinko, who started his career in the late 1980s at the venerable investment bank Lehman Brothers, which traced its roots to 1850. Lehman has been out of business since declaring bankruptcy in 2008 at the beginning of the Great Recession.

But don't worry about Hlinko. He's doing just fine, having spent the last ten years building his own business by harnessing the power of the internet and new technologies to organize activists around progressive and Democratic Party causes. Through his business Left Action, Hlinko has built an email list of more than 2 million activists and a Facebook page with 1.4 million followers. He uses them to send appeals to activists to rally around causes and political campaigns. Sometimes, he asks people on his lists to sign petitions or letters to legislators, or to donate to candidates or causes. Other times, he tries to build opposition to what he calls "right-wing craziness." And in the new world of

politics and activism, clients such as candidates and issue advocacy groups are happy to pay him to tap into his network.

"I understand the challenges and problems with technology"
and the displacement it can cause, Hlinko said. "But here I am, a
simple schmo, sitting here in D.C., able to reach millions of voters. It's amazing."

Hlinko left Lehman to do graduate work at the John F. Ken-
nedy School of Government at Harvard University. After graduate school, he worked with the progressive group MoveOn.org in
its early days and with an online public affairs company. He also
created the ActForLove.org website, a dating site for activists
that promised the opportunity to "take action, get action." He
launched Hlinko Consulting and Left Action in 2009.

Along the way, he founded DraftWesleyClark.com in 2003
to persuade the former U.S. Army general to run for president.
Clark eventually entered the race, and although his candidacy
didn't succeed, it showed Hlinko the power of internet-based
campaigns to influence politics. Hlinko contributed to a similar
effort to drum up advance support for Barack Obama before he
entered the 2008 presidential race.

"When we did the Clark campaign, Facebook and YouTube
didn't even exist," he said. "It's amazing how fast this stuff is
moving." In the not-so-distant past, he recalls, it would cost a
campaign a lot of time and resources to process a $5 donation,
so campaigns relied on larger donations. Today, through the
internet and new processing techniques, this $5 contribution is
valuable, especially when you can multiply the $5 times thou-
sands of supporters. "That showed me that small donors were
going to be the future of politics," he said.

To deliver those activists and potential donors to his clients,
Hlinko spends a lot of time and effort curating his lists to ensure
he is reaching out to people who are likely to respond. He estimates about 1.2 million of the 2 million names on his lists are
regularly active. And he invests in back-end support systems that
maintain the list and let people opt out if they want. He sends

out regular communications to people on the lists to inform them of current events, point out an interesting opinion-page piece, or just to entertain them.

But most important, he wants to keep them engaged, using a light touch he describes as a combination of "humor, edginess, and sometimes downright immaturity." His 2012 book, *Share, Retweet, Repeat: Get Your Message Read and Spread*, was ranked by Amazon as the number one "hot new release" in both web marketing and retail categories.

He said he "absolutely could not" do what he's doing without new technologies that have rolled out in recent years. "In the '60s, '70s, '80s, there literally wouldn't have been a way to do this," he said. "I can be getting on a plane and stop to send out an email to 1.2 million people. That just blows my mind when I imagine what is possible. Or if someone needs to reach 10,000 Alaskans, we can reach them from D.C. The ability to reach people beyond your geographic locale was nearly impossible" in earlier days, he said.

He compares what he does to the old-world matchmaking services of a yenta and imagines trying to explain his work to his departed grandfather, an immigrant from Slovakia who worked in coal mines and later as a bootlegger. "His mind would be blown by it," and especially by the technology that makes it possible, Hlinko said. "I feel like I can do a lot with my little niche. I'm a yenta—with a cause."

He's also not alone in creating new ways of working. As the late American economist Alan Krueger found, 94% of the 10 million jobs created between 2005 and 2015 were not traditional jobs, including more than 60% of positions that went to independent contractors, freelancers, and contract company workers.[7] The way most of us are used to thinking about jobs—working for a single employer, being compensated with a salary and benefits, and changing jobs only infrequently (because it looks bad when people change jobs too often)—is not the reality for many workers today, if not most. How to assure these new ways of organizing work provide stability and dignity to workers, as well as opportunities to do human work, is a major challenge.

Part of what's driving the growth of independent work arrangements is the fact more work is being organized around shorter-term projects. The ability to match the changing skill requirements of work to the talent of workers is attractive to employers. But worker preference is another important consideration. A study of independent workers by the McKinsey Global Institute found 20% to 30% of all workers across the United States and European Union, a political and economic union of nearly thirty countries mostly located in Europe, are involved in independent work—considerably higher than most realize, because employment data do not do a very good job of capturing nontraditional work arrangements. Seventy percent of independent workers are doing so out of preference and not necessity—either to supplement their income or as their primary way to earn a living.

Independent workers also report higher levels of job satisfaction across the board compared with workers in traditional jobs. They like the flexibility in terms of working hours, work location, and choice of projects. Perhaps surprisingly, independent workers believe they receive more recognition for their work and have more opportunities to "learn, grow, and develop." Perhaps unsurprisingly, they also like their bosses more. It is only with income security (not level of income) and access to benefits that they are less satisfied, and these by very small margins.[8]

To a certain extent, the rise of independent work represents a return to older, pre-industrial modes of working. However, this new work is also being supported, and to a certain extent driven, by the development of new digital platforms. While Uber gets all the attention, platforms such as freelance.com directly match workers to projects, and others such as Etsy allow people to market the products of their work directly to potential customers. And then there's Alibaba, the world's largest B2B platform, which effectively allows anyone with an idea for a product to set up a global supply chain to manufacture it.

These new models of employment may, at their best, represent the emergence of a new "people-centered economy."[9] This idea was first proposed by an unlikely duo of big thinkers, Vint Cerf and David Nordfors. Cerf is a technology guru credited with the creation of the TCP/IP internet protocol, and Nordfors is a quantum physicist and data scientist. Together, they crafted this notion over the course of several years of conversation, and then crowdsourced it with a diverse group of thinkers from different fields of work. I was among those involved.

The potential of the people-centered economy is to shift power away from employers to workers by allowing them to choose the work arrangements that best meet their needs for income, employment conditions, job satisfaction, and anything else that is important to them. The emergence of this worker-driven employment market mirrors the shift in marketplace power away from producers and to consumers. Just as producers must compete for consumers in increasingly open markets, so also must employers compete in a market increasingly driven by worker needs and desires. This has important implications for how work is organized, delivered, and paid for.

Certainly, for some, the disappearance of traditional employment has created opportunities for flexible work arrangements, greater control and autonomy, and even a higher income. But for others, it has produced anxiety, instability, and a reduced income and quality of life. We will see which outcome becomes dominant in the future, but whether we like it or not, this is the way our economy works today, and it is likely to be even more true in the future.

The reality is people must have more control over their work—what they do, who they do it for, and with an ability to better define the conditions under which they do it. Of course, millions of people have always worked this way—they are small business owners, tradespeople and artisans, entrepreneurs, and many professionals. But all of us need to be prepared not just to survive in this kind of environment, but to thrive in it.

Human Work and the Knowledge Curve

With all these changes in work, what people need to know and learn is changing—and changing dramatically. We have always known the best way to prepare people for the future is by expanding and developing their talents through formal learning, whether through educational institutions or the many types of worker training programs. While this is still true, the facts on the ground about what people need to be prepared for have radically changed in just the last few years and will change even faster in the future. The world has become far more complex, perhaps even chaotic, because of the massive growth in human knowledge.

R. Buckminster Fuller, a futurist and celebrated inventor who died in the 1980s, first identified what he called the "knowledge doubling curve"—the idea human knowledge expands at an ever-increasing pace. The statistics used to support this concept are dramatic and perhaps a bit fanciful. According to the noted AI researcher and data scientist Feras Batarseh, from the beginning of recorded history until about 1900, human knowledge doubled approximately every hundred years; by 1950, it was doubling every twenty-five years; by 2000, it was doubling every year; and now it may be doubling every day.[10] Even though Batarseh doesn't cite any evidence to support this claim, and freely admits it's difficult to define what it even means, it's not hard to understand why the idea is so popular—it *feels* like what we are experiencing. Certainly, the amount of information and data are growing exponentially, and human knowledge keeps advancing in all fields.

Although the expansion of knowledge is a factor, equally important is that knowledge can rapidly become obsolete. Management consultant Marc Rosenberg talks about the "half-life of knowledge"—the idea that the length of time a lot of information is useful is shrinking at an ever-increasing rate. He described the resulting conundrum like this: "When knowledge is doubling exponentially, yet the useful lifespan of that knowledge is decreasing significantly, the result is a knowledge tsunami—a seemingly unstoppable wave of new information pushing you forward, combined with an extremely forceful undertow of information that used to be valuable but is now just knowledge clutter, pulling you back."[11]

As it happens, there is now hard data to support the hypothesis that knowledge obsolescence is an important factor in careers. As is commonly known, science, technology, engineering, and mathematics (STEM) majors make considerably more money after graduation than non-STEM majors, reflecting the high demand for STEM workers in the economy. However, David Deming and Kadeem Noray of Harvard University discovered that the premium for STEM majors evaporates with time—half of the premium disappears within the decade after graduation, in large part because STEM majors leave their fields at a much faster rate than other graduates. In the words of the authors:

> STEM graduates in applied subjects such as engineering and computer science earn higher wages initially, because they learn job-relevant skills in school. Yet over time, new technologies replace the skills and tasks originally learned by older graduates, causing them to experience flatter wage growth and eventually exit the STEM workforce. Faster technological progress creates a greater sense of shortage, but it is the new STEM skills that are scarce, not the workers themselves.[12]

Whatever the correct numbers are, it's certainly true that in a world where human knowledge is increasing so fast—and rapidly becoming obsolete—there is simply no way we can prepare humans for work in this new age using old models of learning based on mastery of knowledge. Far from being the destroyer of work that it is often portrayed as, AI and other technologies are in fact creating numerous opportunities—if people can take advantage of them. But that's a big if. Large numbers of people are not adequately prepared for human work. Even worse is the reality that our systems for education, training, and employment are not yet aligned with the needs of an economy and society based on human work. That's understandable—they were designed for a different set of circumstances and worked well in their time. But they don't work now, and we face an urgent need to remake them—not least to help those people who are still without work since the pandemic brought a lengthy economic expansion to a sudden and dramatic end.

Wide Learning

Earlier I mentioned robotics expert Ken Goldberg. He has, I believe, an important insight about how AI and the expansion of knowledge affect the way we should think about and prepare people for the work of the future. Goldberg talks about the complementarity of artificial and human intelligence and suggests that instead of replacing people, robots will work with human workers in new ways.[13]

Much of the progress in robotics and artificial intelligence is based on the development of deep learning—a technique in which computers learn through algorithms that methodically drill down into large data sets. Goldberg suggests that humans adopt a complementary approach that he calls "wide learning." Wide learning highlights three dimensions of learning that can expand existing approaches to human learning.

One dimension of wide learning is time. The term of art for educators has been "lifelong learning" for the past couple of decades. I'll return to my concerns about the phrase "lifelong learning" later in the book, but for now let's just say that lifelong learning really expresses only one element of the more inclusive term "wide learning." Certainly, the notion that learning must take place in a wide time context, over the course of people's entire lifetimes, is essential to human work. But so, too, are the other two core dimensions of wide learning.

The second dimension of wide learning is the people doing the learning. Human work must serve a wide range of people, diverse in terms of race, ethnicity, gender, immigration status, and a host of other factors. Human workers must represent the breadth of society for all of us to share in the benefits of their human work.

The third dimension is the content of the learning. What people must learn to be successful in the human work ecosystem represents a wide array of human traits and capabilities. As Goldberg explained, "Much of education today still emphasizes conformity, obedience, and uniformity. Today, the goal is to evolve the way we learn to emphasize the uniquely human skills that AI and robots cannot replicate: creativity, curiosity, imagination, empathy, human communication, diversity, and innovation."

The Skills for Human Work

For wide learning, the content we need to focus on is the skills that human work requires. In this book, I often call them higher-level skills, but others call them "soft skills," "critical-thinking skills," "generic skills" (a term I detest because it reminds me of generic products, which are noteworthy mainly for being cheap), or something else. I prefer the term "higher-level skills" because they are, in fact, at a higher level on recognized taxonomies of learning than basic or purely technical skills.[14]

A simple search online turns up what seems an endless number of articles telling job seekers that these skills are now essential to success, but everyone seems to have a different way not just to name them but also to define and describe them. Almost always, they're offered as a laundry list including everything from communication and problem solving to teamwork and a strong work ethic. People may assume the nature of these nontechnical skills is self-evident, but if they are truly essential to the future of work, the fact that they are so loosely defined is a big problem.

Human work draws upon three sets of skills that everyone needs to develop to a greater or lesser extent: people skills, problem-solving skills, and integrative skills. Let's look at each.

1. People Skills.

As we've already noted, the idea that human work involves interaction with people is a key to understanding its future. While AI will allow many more tasks to be automated, it will also create new capabilities, products, and services—most of which we can't yet imagine. But these innovations will increase the importance of person-to-person relationships, not decrease them. Indeed, AI makes the ability to engage and interact with people even more valuable.

Consider banks. Years ago, people went to a bank when they needed cash. ATMs took over dispensing cash, and now cash itself is being replaced by smartcards and smartphones. I wave my phone at a little black box and the barista hands over my double-tall, half-caf latte with a smile. More to the point, people can go online to move money between accounts, pay bills, and do most of what we used to need to go to the bank to do. But banks—physical offices with customers and tellers in them—haven't gone away. People still go to banks for more complex interactions that can't be done online, and sometimes just because they'd rather interact with a person. Bank tellers don't really exist anymore. The person behind the counter is now a customer service representative who serves as the person-to-person interface between human customers and the full range of financial services the bank offers.

The skills this job requires include an element of technical knowledge, especially of the bank's systems. But mostly, it requires people skills. Communication is one of these skills because it leads to the bank's understanding the customer's needs and the customer's understanding what the bank can do to meet them.

All human work requires people skills, with communication and teamwork chief among them. But I believe there is an even more basic people skill that underlies the others: empathy. It may seem odd to describe empathy as a skill—most see it as a personality trait or even something innate to the person. But empathy leads to the ability to understand and relate to people, and because of that, it has a lot of value in the world of human work.

2. Problem-Solving Skills.

Problem solving is always on the lists of skills people will need for the future of work, but it is seldom explained. Perhaps that's because problem-solving is really a complex, multistage process built on the integration of other, more basic skills. The first stage is identifying or diagnosing the problem—whether it's what a customer really needs from a bank, why a hospital patient is in distress, how a computerized machine tool fell out of tolerances, or what police practices could reduce crime in a neighborhood. To do this, people need to be able to analyze situations with data, insights gathered from personal interactions, or whatever other information is at their disposal. Developing a solution to the problem—solving it—requires subject-matter or technical expertise and the ability to think creatively about how it might be addressed.

Like communication, effectiveness in problem solving requires a certain orientation to the world: attention, certainly, and curiosity. And like empathy, these personality traits are also fundamental skills that are essential for human work.

3. Integrative Skills.

We use higher-level skills alongside technical skills and knowledge that are needed for work in a particular setting. Everyone needs both—engineers, bankers, bakers, teachers, even politicians all need unique sets of technical skills and knowledge coupled with higher-level skills and abilities to do human work.

In a world where human work is constantly changing—and is inherently unpredictable—it's not either/or. Everyone needs a combination of both general and technical learning. These skills are not applied in isolation. What's important to human work is integrating them.

Because of the ever-changing nature of work and society and the fact that people need to keep learning throughout their lives, the ability to learn is an essential skill for human work. Learning is an integrative skill—in this case, the ability to integrate new learning with what we already know and can do. In the world of human work, people also need to learn quickly and purposefully, so literacy—both quantitative and verbal—is an essential building block everyone needs to support ongoing and continuous learning throughout life. Here, too, creativity is essential, as is another trait too often undervalued: humility.

These skills for human work are quite different from the ones required for work in more industrial-age settings, which means that the way we develop people's skills through education and training will need to change. These changes will be described in the next chapter.

Human Work and Wide Learning

Marcus Dodson's résumé tells a story of the changes in the U.S. economy in recent years, including the loss of good jobs in long-standing industries such as manufacturing. But it also shows how wide learning can create new opportunities for people to thrive in a world of human work.

Dodson worked for a denim apparel company that, like many others in that industry, moved its production to Mexico after the North American Free Trade Agreement took effect—in Dodson's case, from Kentucky. Another employer, an auto parts producer, shifted production from western Kentucky to plants in China, Mexico, Poland, and Spain. And he also worked for a manufacturer of home oil heating pumps, once made in Kentucky and now produced in France.

Fortunately, Dodson's story, unlike that of many others, did not end there. He decided back in 2008, when the Great Recession hit, that he "didn't necessarily want to go to China to work." So he started looking for a position that promised longevity and predictability and for an employer that wasn't going to outsource its work or move out of the country. As an information technology specialist, it wouldn't have been surprising if he found work in a start-up or growing company in the technology sector, but instead he went to work for the state of Tennessee.

Dodson, then 37, took a pay cut of more than $10,000 when he first joined state government, but he quickly decided he had made the right decision. "I knew in my first seven days of employment here that I was into something big," he said. He quickly moved up from an information resource specialist, installing and maintaining computer hardware and software, to a series of supervisory positions. He enjoyed the challenge of "always looking for a way to deliver a better product or service to a constituent," whether that was a coworker in state government or a taxpayer interacting with the government.

While the work energized him, the learning opportunities Tennessee state government provides for its employees excited him. "Hey, I knew I needed learning and development," he said. After several years of trying, Dodson was admitted to the Tennessee Government Management Institute and the LEAD Tennessee programs. Those programs "opened my eyes up to the fact that for a true leader, it's not just about you. It's about helping others around you to succeed," Dodson said. With more education and training came more promotions. Dodson, now in his late forties, has advanced from a supervisory to a managerial role, overseeing twelve employees on the state Department of Treasury information systems team.

And he's not finished learning. Taking advantage of the state government's program that covers an employee's tuition for one class per semester at a state institution, Dodson completed a master's degree at Tennessee State University. As the first in his family to go to college, graduating from Western Kentucky University in 1995, Dodson feels a sense of pride in his own accomplishments and gratitude for how his new employer offers what he calls "a culture of continuous learning." "I get excited talking about training and development," Dodson said. "And I just love coming to work. ... I plan on staying here until they have to carry me out."

Dodson's story offers many lessons about what is happening to work. He got his good job because of his solid background in technology, but the job wasn't in what we typically associate with the technology sector. In fact, 90% of IT job openings are in non–tech industry sectors such as financial services, health care, and professional services, and IT jobs in those other sectors are growing 50% faster than in the tech sector.[15] Because of his broad range of skills, knowledge, and abilities—and because his employer gave him opportunities to further develop them—his job soon grew to involve much more than technical expertise. Dodson's work now is as much about people skills such as leadership as it is about technology.

We can learn a lot from Marcus Dodson—about how people need to adapt to changes in the economy, about what our education systems need to do to remain relevant, and about how employers need to think differently vis-à-vis their role as learning organizations. His is a story about human work, what it looks like and how it's different. Instead of a race to the bottom, where work built on repetitive tasks is done by the cheapest possible labor until it can be automated, human work engages people in doing things only humans can do.

His story also shows the importance of wide learning to develop both the technical and people skills to do the human work his new job requires. It shows how the essential nature of human work involves engagement with others and our most human traits—qualities such as empathy and compassion.

Much of what has been written about work in the coming years starts from the assumption millions of jobs will be lost as a result of technology and draws from the conclusion work is somehow going away for many people. Dodson's experience tells a different story. The beginning of his journey is familiar to millions of American workers. But his path of continuous talent development has paid off in important ways. This is the story of work that should be told more often.

As a society, we must now undertake the massive effort necessary to make wide learning a reality by assuring everyone has the chance to develop the ability to do human work in any chosen profession. Human work requires us to rethink every aspect of how we provide everyone the opportunity to learn, because the individual—the *learner*—must be at the center of the system.

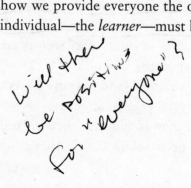

Preparing for the Work of the Future

"Your future hasn't been written yet. No one's has. Your future is whatever you make it. So make it a good one."
—Doc Brown, *Back to the Future Part III*, 1990

Marcia McCallum spent nearly three decades working as a waitress to help support her family and being "your typical soccer mom," ferrying her four children to practices, games, and school events. In 2012, she decided to pursue her ambition to become a nurse, and to reach her objective, she enrolled in community college twenty-nine years after graduating from high school.

Her first experiences at Austin Community College in Texas were both humorous and challenging. Students thought McCallum was registering her child for classes when she stood in line for a student ID, and other students believed she was a professor when she showed up in her first classes. And in her first class, a summer-session course in elementary algebra, she realized how much math she had forgotten. Her oldest daughter, Ashton, helped her by making flash cards to refresh Marcia's memory. Her other children—daughters Jordan and Megan and son Jon— were also very supportive.

"They were maybe a little skeptical, but once I got into the second and third semesters, they were my biggest cheerleaders," said McCallum, who separated from the children's father.

She continued to work as she moved toward becoming a full-time student. This meant a daunting schedule with a full-time course load and waitressing three days a week, with double shifts on Saturdays and Sundays. McCallum was studying to become a nurse, but after her first taste of work in a laboratory, she decided to switch her major to biotechnology, and she started to excel as a student. "I decided I don't agree with the 'C's get degrees,'" she said. "I believe you need to get your A game up there and get some A's."

By 2016, McCallum had earned an associate degree in applied science and technology. She also helped Austin Community College set up its Bioscience Incubator lab and worked part-time with a start-up biotech company in Austin. Now in her mid-50s, seven years after restarting her education, McCallum has another associate degree in general science and works full-time for another biotechnology company, helping to grow cell cultures that eventually will be harvested for therapeutic antibodies to help treat cancer, inflammatory conditions, infectious diseases, and dermatological problems.

"Sometimes I have to pinch myself that I'm in on something like this," she said. "I was finally able to stop waiting tables. It's been quite a journey. I just feel so lucky."

Now, with a full-time job with benefits, McCallum is hoping to save enough money to buy a house that can be a gathering place for her family, which now includes four grandchildren and four very proud children. "Seeing my mom go through school after having raised four kids and essentially starting over is a kind of testament to how hard work and persistence can really pay off," said Jon McCallum, Marcia's son. "From what I can tell and can see, she's a success, no matter how long it took."

The Global Talent Gap

While McCallum's is an inspiring story, it is becoming a more familiar one as millions of people across the globe seek to find their place in a changing economy by upgrading their talents or developing new ones. It's not hard to understand why. The transformation of the workforce is real, but the headline that it is leading to job losses is not. The reality is there is a growing global shortage of talent, creating challenges for the economy and society but opportunities for those with talent that is in demand.

A 2018 study by Korn Ferry predicts that, in the absence of action to better develop and use talent, the global talent shortage will reach more than 85.2 million people by 2030, costing a staggering $8.5 trillion in unrealized economic activity. This shortage will hit the United States particularly hard—the study predicts $1.7 trillion of the global shortfall from worker shortages will be in the United States, representing fully 6% of the economy. Human work represents a shift away from repetitive tasks—the work machines can do—and toward a new focus on higher-level thinking and human traits. None of this means work for people is disappearing. Quite the opposite is true.

Recent U.S. data show that today we are facing an unprecedented gap between the demand for skills and their availability in workers. These gaps will only grow more pronounced as hazardous, repetitive jobs such as meatpacking are automated as the economy recovers from the COVID-19 recession. In December 2007, at the onset of the Great Recession, there were 1.7 unemployed people for every job opening in the United States. A surplus of workers over available jobs was the historical norm, but when the Great Recession took hold, this ratio exploded—reaching a peak of 6.4 unemployed people for every job opening in July 2009. Some feared this would become the new normal, but something else quite unexpected happened.

First, job openings eventually returned to their pre-recession levels, although it took until August 2014 for them to do so. But they didn't stop there. In December 2018, the U.S. economy reached a point there were more job openings than unemployed people—700,000 openings and 630,000 unemployed—for the first time in the nation's history.[1] But if there were so many job openings, why were people still unemployed?

As we saw in Chapter 1, most jobs created since the end of the Great Recession require learning beyond high school. Unemployment today—whether it's joblessness among people counted in official statistics or people who have stopped looking for work entirely—is generally a result of a lack of skills necessary to pursue the opportunities for work that exists in the labor market. If automation through AI is eliminating jobs, there is almost no evidence of it happening in today's economy.

But Marcia McCallum's story also points to a big reason we are having such a hard time closing the global talent gap. While mistaking a new student for a professor is amusing and not a big deal, especially in a community college that is working hard to meet her needs, it's still true that she entered a system that isn't designed for McCallum and people like her. Attitudes toward learning are changing as more people experience the shifts taking place throughout the world, and they expect our education systems to keep up. Most people now recognize that education is no longer something that people only do only when they're young and before they enter their careers.

Even though we still consider students such as McCallum "nontraditional," most Americans, 59%, already believe education is something that happens throughout life. An even larger percentage of people in other countries and regions believe it: 63% in South Africa, 64% in Canada, 66% in Latin America, and 70% in China. These countries also have the highest proportions of people who believe workers need to keep learning or retraining throughout their careers to stay up-to-date.[2]

But naysayers continue to insist the talent gap is a myth. On the one hand, they argue that increased demand for learning represented by degrees and other credentials awarded after high school is caused solely by opportunistic employers taking advantage of buyer's markets to impose tougher requirements on workers.[3] These naysayers fail to see the contradiction when they also argue that economic cycles produce periods such as the one that began in 2011, after the Great Recession, in which unemployment declined to near-record lows. But whether they argue that either an oversupply or undersupply of workers is evidence of this "myth," at best these dismissals are wishful thinking about what is really happening to jobs. In my view, they represent instead an unwillingness to accept the implications of the broad demand for talent that is developed through formal learning and experience.

Under the patronizing headline "Two Tacos and a B.A., Please," *The Wall Street Journal* seized on recent research as proof that skill demands are not increasing. But the study they cite actually proved the opposite—it showed that even during the height of the Great Recession, no more than 25% of the increase in skills demanded by employers was a result of the increased availability of workers.[4] The researchers found actual changes in the skills required to do tasks associated with jobs are what's actually driving the need for more learning after high school. Increasing skill demands and the resultant skills gaps are facts of life in today's economy. The "sugar high" of low unemployment during good economic times only masks the truth about labor market demand. When the economy is bad, employers overwhelmingly choose people with the highest levels of talent, and companies are willing to pay a premium in wages and benefits to get the best talent.

The False Dichotomy between Education and Training

Of course, the global demand for skills and the emergence of human work are placing enormous pressure on the way we prepare people for work and life. Understanding how human work is different is the key to figuring out what we need to do to adapt our learning systems. Unfortunately, the way we are accustomed to thinking about education and training is getting in the way of the solutions we need.

For example, we tend to believe some work requires a specific set of technical knowledge and skills that people should learn in the fastest possible ways. We have a process for that. It's called workforce training, and it functioned reasonably well before the acceleration of demands for talent fundamentally changed, especially in the aftermath of the 2008 recession. And then there's another kind of learning—one we like to believe is at a higher level—that prepares people for life beyond work. We call this education. In fact, many people believe education at its highest level isn't about work at all, which somehow makes it more ... pure.

For the most part, education and workforce training are treated as fundamentally different activities. Different systems provide them, and whatever learning people obtain from one system is not recognized in the other. I often hear academics say they are educators and not trainers, and sometimes they even go so far as to say, "You train a dog, not a person." While this is an extreme view, the underlying message is education and training don't mix.

If anything, too much of what the public sees in today's higher education model looks like job training—for academics. It comes across as the perpetuation of techniques and strategies that bear little resemblance to the realities of modern work and life. Fairly or not, this exacerbates the view that college isn't about preparing people for "real-world" work opportunities.

This may be a case of well-intended people on both sides of this artificial divide talking past one another. A good example from earlier in the decade arose in the aftermath of the global Great Recession in the United Kingdom, when the government crafted a white paper on higher education aimed at better linking employability and education.[5] The government seized on near-term data showing a lack of labor market integration of recent graduates, while the academic community responded with skepticism about the wisdom of such "shortsighted" thinking.

"Employability of graduates is a shared responsibility between employers and universities, but you really have to consider whether you are in the business of preparing students for their first job or for lifelong careers," said Professor John Brennan, who directed the Centre for Higher Education Research and Information at the Open University. This perceived dichotomy between short-term training for jobs and longer-term education for life is at the heart of the ongoing debate, but in many ways, it's based on a false premise.[6]

In preparing people for human work, it's obvious neither training devoid of broader learning nor education devoid of preparation for work will give people what they need. Indeed, this deeply held belief that education and workforce training are different breaks down. To tell the truth, I'm not sure it was ever valid. What we need is wide learning—a broad, integrated system focused on individual learners.

In Chapter 2, I examined the emerging occupations representing examples of human work, the Helpers, Bridgers, Integrators, and Creators. But as those examples make clear, human work requires higher-level thinking skills and focuses more on human-centered tasks such as assisting and caring for others, maintaining relationships, and thinking creatively. Preparing people to do human work is not just a matter of identifying growth occupations and training people in the technical skills they require. The word that comes to mind when I look at these occupations is *breadth*—human work requires a breadth of talent that tasks that can be automated do not. All this points toward something very important about how to prepare people for a future of human work and suggests some of the ways our learning systems are inadequate to the demands human work places on them. Developing higher-level thinking and our most human traits will need to be central to the new system of learning that will emerge in the coming decades.

The Contemporary Problem with "Training"

Throughout the world, sizable and elaborate education and training systems prepare people for work and life. To a very large extent, they work very well and effectively meet the needs of millions and will be the foundation upon which a new learning system for human work will be built.

But there are problems with these systems, too—problems that relate to the disconnect between the environment they were created for and the one in which we live today. These problems will grow more severe in the future of human work.

Let's start with what has generally been called training. Of course, training is a part of virtually all jobs—even if it's as simple as a new worker learning a company's processes or being "broken in" by an old hand. But a lot of training is designed to do more. In an industrial-age economy, the skills needed to do a lot of jobs can be learned in a short time and by anyone with a modicum of "basic knowledge"—literacy and numeracy—and a good attitude and work ethic. The United States, like other countries around the world, offers these short-term training programs through a large and complex workforce development system involving local governments, unions, industry groups, public and private training providers, and many other actors.

The problem is they often don't work. As one example, an evaluation of a U.S. program to retrain workers whose jobs went overseas found that after four years, only 37% of participants were still working in the industry they had been trained for.[7]

The reasons these and other training programs are struggling in today's environment are not hard to understand. For starters, they are much smaller than they used to be and nowhere near the size needed to meet the needs of today's economy, much less the future's. Funding for the core federal workforce development program in the United States[8] has been cut from $4.62 billion in the 2001 budget year to $2.79 billion in the 2019 budget year.[9]

But the real problems run even deeper. When these programs were designed, recessions caused people to lose jobs, but as the economy recovered, most workers were able to return to their old jobs or one in a similar company or industry. As we learned in 2008, recessions now wipe out entire industries, and the jobs available in the recovery may be completely different from the ones lost. Another problem is more jobs—and almost all good jobs—require a range of higher-level knowledge, skills, and abilities that cannot be learned in the short time frame of most job-training programs.

Yet another problem is in today's environment—and even more so in the future—the learning people need requires the integration of both technical and higher-level thinking skills that can only be built on a strong foundation of general learning. The jobs that are unlikely to be automated require more than a narrow set of technical skills. For example, a growing number of jobs require integrating technical skills and knowledge with strong interpersonal communication capability and personal attributes such as empathy. This is true for work that involves dealing with clients or the public, but also for the many jobs that involve supervision or team leadership.

Still other jobs require coupling advanced technical skills with analytical thinking and problem solving. Many jobs in advanced manufacturing and information technology fall into this category. While we may believe these high-skill jobs are purely technical, a closer examination shows the actual work is analytical—diagnosing a problem and devising what is often a highly creative solution. Employers and providers can't just train people in narrow sets of technical skills for the human work these jobs represent.

Is College the Answer?

Given the demand for learning in today's economy and the challenges faced by the current training system, it's no wonder colleges and universities are playing an increasingly important role in preparing people for work. Of course, this role is nothing new—since the first clergyman graduated from Harvard, workforce development has always been an important role of higher education.

As Marcia McCallum's story illustrates so well, colleges and universities are avenues of opportunity for millions. In the

United States, community colleges are essential in offering people the opportunity to gain the knowledge, skills, and abilities they need. Some still call them the best-kept secret in higher education or believe they are poorly understood and underappreciated. I'm not sure this is true. Community colleges enroll more than a third of all college students, and 83% of Americans hold a favorable view of them—much higher than hold a favorable view of bachelor's-granting colleges and universities (69%) or the higher education system as a whole (55%).[10]

Some people continue to insist that Americans are concerned about the quality of community college education. But when it comes to the value of the credentials that community colleges offer—the truest measure of quality—there is no evidence to support this concern. While an overwhelming majority of Americans (70%) believe a bachelor's degree is "worth the investment and usually pays off," a virtually equal proportion (69%) believe this of associate degrees, and 90% believe it of vocational and technical certificates.[11]

On the other hand, the role bachelor's-granting institutions play in preparing people for work may indeed be poorly understood and underappreciated. The number-one reason people decide to go to college is to "improve my employment opportunities": 91% of prospective U.S. students believe this is important.[12] An equal 91% of Americans say college graduates should be able to get jobs paying more than high school graduates earn.[13] In spite of this obvious and overwhelming factor, the view that bachelor's-granting colleges are not about preparing people to land good jobs and have satisfying careers dies hard.

When I talk to people who embrace this idea—and I've talked to a lot of them—they always express their concerns in terms of the "true purpose" of higher education being about something other than work. I've heard everything from "the life of the mind" or "broadening your perspectives." Frankly, work and a job are seen at best as necessary evils and at worst as distractions from what really matters.

Of course, the reality on campuses is quite different, and colleges and universities that award bachelor's degrees play a central role in preparing people for careers. More bachelor's degrees are awarded in business than in any other field, followed by health professions.[14] At least two-thirds of bachelor's degrees are awarded in fields that are obviously related to specific industries or occupations (such as engineering, agriculture, computer and information sciences, and many more), and this is not even counting fields with excellent career prospects such as mathematics and physical and biological sciences.

But I must acknowledge, people who insist a college education should be broadening and include more than preparation for a specific career have a point. Human work, by its nature of earning, learning, and serving, engages our full range of abilities and capabilities.

Toward a New Learning System

Yet there are some basic problems with relying on higher education as it is now to meet the needs of a future of human work:

- Far more people need the higher-level learning required by human work than our systems are equipped to serve, and people need this learning throughout their lives.

- Our education systems, including the colleges and universities that make up what we generally regard as higher education, do not do a good enough job of developing the skills human work requires, in large part because their efforts too often are divorced from the settings in which human work is actually performed.

- Not nearly enough is known about what the graduates of our education systems actually know and can do—least of all by the graduates themselves.

Let's look at each problem in turn and examine how a new learning system could solve it.

1. *More people need higher-level learning.*

The first problem is too few people advance to the levels of talent required by human work. This problem is only going to get worse. We now expect everyone to at least finish high school, but high school is no longer enough. Already the labor market demands continual learning after high school because work is changing in ways that increase the demand for these skills. But it's not enough that everyone obtains some education or training after high school. The constantly changing technical skills in demand in the economy mean workers need to reskill and up-skill more frequently in today's economy, so everyone must continue learning throughout life. This doesn't mean people will keep going back to school every few years (although many will), but it does mean the days of once-and-done education are over.

But much of the existing education systems were designed to meet the needs of students and a society that no longer exist. These systems were designed for what we all believe is the normal way for people to get higher education.

On the well-trod School-College-Work pathway, we assume after graduating from high school at the age of 17 or 18, young people should enroll in college. Because we believe almost everyone wants a bachelor's degree, most enroll in a university—the best one they can afford and get into. There are a lot of choices of where to go to college, and we know parents take prospective students on college visits and family and friends help them make the decision about where to go. Of course, we know there are some students who can't afford a university, or whose grades aren't good enough, but we assume most of these students can go to a community college—either to "pick up a trade" or to save money for a couple years before transferring to a university.

Once in college, we assume most students go full-time and that most graduate in four years unless they change majors or fail some courses. Many live on campuses or nearby unless they can't afford to, in which case they live with their parents as "commuter students."

While we know affordability is a big problem, we assume parents pay the bulk of college expenses and, when they can't, that financial aid and loans make up the difference. While some students work during the summer to help pay for college, we believe most have an internship (the motivated ones), travel, or goof off.

We also believe the final step on the School-College-Work pathway happens after graduation (even if it's put off for a few years for graduate or professional school or a "gap year"), when graduates begin their careers.

Almost every assumption above is false as it relates to today's students. Using the common definition of traditional students as those who start college directly after high school, don't have dependents, attend full-time, and either don't work or work part-time, only one in four students is traditional.[15] Half of all students are financially independent of their parents—Mom and Dad are not helping them out, at least not financially. Four out of ten are employed full-time. Six out of ten live on their own—not with their parents or on campus. A quarter have dependents of their own. What all this means is today's students have complex lives, not least because they are already working long before they graduate college—they have no choice.

The older students are, the less well the higher education system works for them. More than a third of today's college students are older than 25—around 7 million of them. This may seem surprising given the assumption of many people that college is something for the young. But what's really surprising is the number of older students is in fact very low compared to the number of adults who need learning and credentials after high school. More than 163 million Americans are between the ages of 25 and 64, meaning no more than 4% of them are enrolled in college at any given time. Given that most jobs being created today require a college degree or other quality credential, the fact so few adults are enrolled in programs of study that lead to them is extremely worrisome. It's a problem both for the future of millions of individuals and the economy.

Marcia McCallum found a community college program that opened the doors to an opportunity she couldn't have imagined, and she made the sacrifices necessary to make it work for her. Unfortunately, the kind of pathway she found isn't readily available for millions of people. Taking education systems that are designed from the ground up for traditional students—to sort winners from losers—and making them effective at helping people develop their knowledge, skills, and abilities for human work is not as simple as adding on a new program for today's students or hiring some new staff members focused on outreach.

But the disconnect between our current systems and what society needs goes much deeper than even the dramatic mismatch between the skill demands of jobs and the skill levels of workers. Some higher education institutions are leading the way by showing how a focus on the success of all students requires a transformation of everything the institution does to become truly learner centered. Bharat Anand, vice provost for advances in learning at Harvard University and a celebrated Harvard Business School professor who created the online platform HBX, said the key to institution-wide transformation is the development of a true "learner-centered" model. To accomplish this at Harvard, Anand led the Business School's digital learning initiative, and he's now been tasked with trying to do so at scale across the university's twelve schools.[16] This is a tall order at the world's most recognized university, but also a sure indication the concept of learner-centeredness has implications even within the lofty realm of Harvard.

A more down-to-earth example is Amarillo College in the Texas Panhandle. When Russell Lowery-Hart arrived to work at the college in 2010, one harsh statistic stared him in the face: a graduation rate of 9%. Clearly, something wasn't working, so he set out to find out why. The answer surprised him.

"When I looked at our success rates, I was embarrassed, so I asked our students what was keeping them from being successful in the classroom. And as a recovering faculty member, I expected academic answers," he said. "What I heard changed who I am, professionally and personally. Because all the issues in the classroom had nothing to do with the classroom. They were all life barriers keeping students from being successful—things such as child care, health care, food, housing, utility payments," he said. "The things we take for granted are actually keeping students from being successful in classrooms across the country." *Buying ones own time*

First as vice president of student affairs and since 2014 as president, Lowery-Hart convened focus groups to gather advice on what the college needed to do to improve completion rates. In the case of a community college, this means having a student finish an associate, or two-year, degree program faster, generally in no more than three years. From students, he learned they wanted a college built on strong relationships with college personnel and good customer service. So Lowery-Hart studied the practices of companies such as Zappos and the Texas-based Happy State Bank, both with reputations for strong customer service. Old ideas about the ivory tower with administrators and staff keeping a certain distance from students went out the window. Lowery-Hart and his senior staff give out their cell phone numbers to everyone—students, parents, staff.

Founded in 1929, Amarillo College now has about 10,000 students, but as Lowery-Hart notes, the profile of the typical student is much different from what it used to be. He often talks of the prototype of today's enrollee at Amarillo—a hypothetical student he calls Maria.

"She's the typical student at Amarillo. She's first generation: 71% of our students are the first in their families to go to college. She goes to school part-time: 52% of our students take twelve hours or less of classwork a year. She's working two part-time jobs. She's a mother and she's 27 years old. And she's smart and ambitious and capable and all we have to do is remove a few key barriers for her to live up to her potential," he said. "A majority of higher ed is set up for the students from the '80s, but today our communities are depending on us to educate the students we have, not the students we wish we had."

Starting nearly a decade ago and accelerating the effort since Lowery-Hart became president, Amarillo College has undertaken a transformative program to address poverty and its effects on student success. Called the No Excuses Poverty Initiative, the program has brought cultural change and sharply improved completion rates to the college in a city of 200,000 with more than 14% of its population living below the poverty level. Lowery-Hart acknowledged that initially "we thought, like a lot of people, that this isn't our mission. The community is supposed to solve those problems. But we're the community college. We had to see our mission in addressing these issues, even if that meant gluing the resources in the community together in a coherent program. We knew we had to do something."

The college established a program to provide student assistance that goes far beyond financial aid. Amarillo has an on-campus resource center with a food pantry and a clothes closet with suits and fancier clothes for students who are going to job interviews and more casual clothing for everyday wear. Toiletries also are available. The social services department finds ways to help students with rent, utility bills, child care expenses, transportation, and legal services. The school has dental, legal, and car repair clinics, where students train while also offering needed assistance to fellow students. The Amarillo College Foundation contributes $60,000 annually to support the programs, and local businesses have entered into partnerships with the center for efforts such as bulk purchases for the food bank. Close to 20% of Amarillo's students receive some of the services.

On the academic side, Amarillo decided to jettison the usual sixteen-week semester and go to a schedule of eight-week sessions. While there has been some grumbling from faculty, students like the shorter, more intense courses, and overall grades have improved under the new schedule. The three-year completion rate now stands at 53%.

Others are starting to pay attention to Amarillo College and places like it. Lowery-Hart has been invited to tell the college's story to the U.S. Senate Committee on Health, Education, Labor, and Pensions. And in 2018, more than thirty institutions from fourteen states attended a conference Lowery-Hart and Amarillo hosted to explain the No Excuses program.

The program is making a difference in individual students' lives, but also in the larger Amarillo community. "This isn't just about doing the right thing for our students. It is about the economic future of our community," Lowery-Hart said. "For every 10% we can increase educational attainment, we get a 22% increase in GDP. So, this isn't about conservative or liberal, Democrat or Republican. This is about the economic future of our community and our country. And until we address poverty as the underlying barrier to education attainment, we're never going to unleash the economic power that exists in our citizens."

President Lowery-Hart recognizes poverty is the real-world face of income inequality and the most difficult problem facing communities such as his. While the causes and solutions are complex, in today's economy the single most important strategy to reduce poverty is to increase the share of people with education or training after high school.

Amarillo College shows wide learning in practice. Officials there have addressed the first element of wide learning—time—by changing the way their programs are organized and scheduled to make them accessible to far more of the adult learners who need them. Their mission focuses all their attention on the second element—people. And they address the third—content—by developing and offering programs that respond to the changing employment needs and opportunities of their region.

Colleges and universities have always known they are important to the nation. Given the demand for talent globally and the role they play as one of the key providers of talent development (but not the only one), they may be more important now than ever. But they also are coming to understand their value lies in the success of the people they serve and not in any intrinsic characteristic of the institution itself. While colleges and universities have taken pride in the success of the students they graduate—as they should—they are also beginning to realize that who they serve is, in fact, the broader community and not just those they enroll and graduate. As we see at Amarillo College, this understanding truly transforms a higher education institution into one whose mission is outwardly focused on the community and broader society.

2. *We don't do a good job developing skills that human work requires.*

Now to the second problem with today's education systems—they don't develop or integrate the wide range of learning needed for human work.

In Chapter 2, I described the skills human work requires—people skills, problem-solving skills, and integrative skills. Sadly, neither our education nor our training systems are designed to really develop these skills. Instead, we tend to think in terms of academic skills and technical skills, and too often expect students to learn them separately.

While all colleges and universities emphasize the importance of such human traits as empathy and ethical behavior, developing them is not done in an intentional way by institutions. Indira Samarasekera, who served as president and vice chancellor of the University of Alberta in Canada from 2005 to 2015, has spoken consistently about the imperative of learning institutions to directly improve the "human traits" of learners to prepare them for the world of work. "Empathy, human emotion, social skills, and things like ethics and morality, character, and kindness are not simply traits you are born with," she told an audience of educators at a meeting I attended in England in 2019. "Universities and colleges have to actually make developing those traits a central part of the curriculum."

None of the skills needed for human work are mysterious—they can be defined, taught, and measured.[17] But you don't learn them by sitting passively in a lecture hall listening to lectures on "Lessons from Great Problem Solvers throughout History." As with any skill, you learn them by doing, which means education for them must be active and engaging. Indeed, one of the best ways to learn skills for human work is by actually doing human work.

I have said human work requires something more than technical skills, no matter how advanced they may be. Unfortunately, a lot of people still believe pushing more people into STEM fields or vocational-technical education is the answer. Indeed, this message has gotten through to learners around the world in a big way. According to OECD, 40% of first-year students in Germany's higher learning sector are focused on the STEM fields, as are 32% of students in Mexico, 31% in South Korea, and 29% in the United Kingdom. The average for all twenty-seven OECD nations was 27%—more than a quarter of all students in the leading economies of the world.[18] But while STEM is frequently touted as the solution to the world's economic maladies, focusing solely on STEM doesn't work. Human work demands a broader, more integrated kind of learning.

But this is not the only problem with a singular focus on STEM. Women, people of color, youth from low-income households are poorly represented in the STEM disciplines, and STEM workers are overwhelmingly male and from higher socioeconomic backgrounds.[19] Women drop out of STEM courses at a rate 50% higher than men. And among those students who do graduate, those from African American and other nonwhite backgrounds are less likely to be employed in their fields of study. None of this is because women or students of color can't perform well in STEM fields or learn STEM skills. But the way we teach them doesn't work for large numbers of students who don't fit the traditional mold. Learning systems that integrate technical and higher-level thinking skills and allow students to develop them through active learning and engagement are a big part of how we eliminate these barriers.

As I described in Chapter 2, the benefits—both to the economy and student—of education in the STEM fields evaporate over time because of the increasingly rapid obsolescence of technical knowledge and skills. This doesn't mean people don't need technical skills, only that they cannot rely on them exclusively for success through life. In the long run, the desire and ability to continuously learn new skills across a range of fields is far more important.[20]

This leads to another piece our education and training systems don't get right. As we saw earlier, human work demands learning across a range of fields. But our education systems are almost always segmented into specific disciplines. Students might major in chemistry or education or psychology with the intention of finding jobs in those fields or related ones, but this is no longer how work is organized. College degrees are supposed to mitigate this problem by having students take courses in a range of disciplines—so-called general education requirements—but unfortunately, taking a smattering of courses in history, biology, and economics to complement an engineering major doesn't really provide the integration of knowledge and skills across fields that human work demands.

A great example of how to integrate learning across disciplines can better prepare people for human work can be found at the University of Virginia. There, medical students study at the university's art museum to hone their observational and diagnostic skills—crucial to their success in the practice of medicine. The required six-week course in art was developed because research showed that medical students and doctors who took part had more capacity for personal reflection, tolerance of ambiguity, and awareness of personal bias. These are very real skills that have big effects on the quality of care their patients will one day receive.[21]

Unfortunately, higher education, even in occupationally focused majors, is often too removed from the settings in which work is actually done. This may not have been a problem when work and education were so distinct. Indeed, some undoubtedly saw it as an advantage. But in a world of human work, this forced separation creates a range of problems. Work offers excellent opportunities for the kind of active, engaged learning that develops higher-level thinking skills and human traits. It's also true when virtually everyone needs to be learning—and learning all the time—a system in which learning and earning are treated as separate activities is frankly unworkable. These two aspects of life are becoming one.

Colleges and universities such as Nashville State Community College in Tennessee, which serves about 10,000 students mostly from a seven-county region in Middle Tennessee, are the kinds of places where serving today's students and preparing them for human work is beginning to take shape. The college offers practical learning opportunities that lead to certificates, associate degrees, and other credentials, very much rooted in the lived experiences of the learners from the region. The college's student profile, about 40% students of color and tilted heavily toward students older than 25, is typical for these kinds of schools.[22] The college has committed itself to supporting students interested in serving as teachers, nurses, health care managers, and other human workers. But the task is not easy, given the complex life circumstances of the students and their prior learning experiences.

"We've got to serve the students we get, not the ones we wish we had," Shanna Jackson, president of Nashville State Community College since 2018, told an audience of my colleagues at Lumina Foundation in 2019. This is the same rationale as Lowery-Hart used in Amarillo. Jackson has made it a major focus of the college to improve student success rates—six-year graduation rates hovered in the low 20% range prior to her arrival—by better matching students with the in-demand, real human skill–driven jobs in the region.

3. We don't know what graduates have learned.

This brings us to the final problem with our current systems for preparing people for human work: no one knows what the graduates of our education systems really know and can do, least of all the graduates themselves.

The solution to this problem is to assure the transparency of learning by defining clear frameworks for knowledge and skills so employers, educators, and student workers themselves are all speaking the same language about skills, are using common definitions for them, and can communicate effectively about what people need to know and be able to do. Transparency about learning can build a much stronger system of credentials and multiple pathways for individuals through learning and careers. In the following chapter, I will describe this system.

Pathways to Learning

While higher education is, and will remain, critically important to preparing people for a future of human work, it's not the only pathway to follow, and a college degree is not the only credential of value in today's economy. There are other pathways to good jobs. For example, certifications are important and valuable non-degree credentials—especially in fields such as IT. But sadly, we tend to exaggerate the availability of pathways to valuable nondegree credentials and the number of people on those pathways. No more than 4% of American adults hold an industry or professional certification with value in the job market as their only credential.[23]

Besides, it's very hard for older workers to obtain the new skills they need for a changing employment market. In Europe, fewer than 11% of adults are engaged in formal education and training. Even less formal learning opportunities, such as on-the-job training that doesn't lead to a recognized credential, are available to too few people and are hardly available to those who need them most, such as the long-term unemployed. In Europe, fewer than 4% of adults who have completed only primary or lower secondary education are enrolled in formal education or training programs.

We should understand and accept that the School-College-Work pathway is largely broken, which may not matter so much because it's obsolete anyway. It no longer describes how people progress through learning and careers, nor does it describe the way our systems of learning and earning should be organized. A 2019 *Harvard Business Review* article may have summed it up best—"College degree programs simply cannot keep pace with how fast things are changing in the workforce."[24] Put another way, human workers need more than the learning they will get through a one-time experience at a fixed point in their lives.

What is needed to prepare people for human work is a new kind of learning system that combines what we now view as education and training, and also integrates the wide range of learning that human work requires—however and wherever it takes place. In this system, the temporal idea of "first you learn, then you work" is replaced by a continuous, integrated model of talent development and deployment. This new approach takes us well beyond the historic concept of "lifelong learning." And this system is large enough to serve everyone who needs to learn, which means everyone.

Human work is profoundly changing the learning needs of society, and it's inevitable that our systems for providing people with learning opportunities must change as well. But just as we're saddled by obsolete notions of what work is all about, the way we think about the purpose of education can hold us back from developing the solutions we need. In Chapter 5, I will describe approaches for bridging the divide between human work and learning.

Building a New System

One person who understands the importance of building a new human work infrastructure is Penny Pritzker, a nationally regarded leader who has worked from several different vantage points to make it happen. Pritzker has started and run several companies in her career, in industries ranging from real estate to financial services to hospitality. She served as U.S. secretary of commerce and has been a major philanthropic investor in organizations developing big new ideas to transform learning at all levels. And she has committed her time and energy to the reform of large, influential education systems as a member of the boards of the Chicago Public Schools and Harvard Corporation.

Pritzker said the learning system needs large-scale, not marginal, change to advance human work. "We've got to execute on all levels to build this future human workforce," Pritzker told me. "It's different than it was before. We have to make sure people have the critical thinking and interpersonal communication skills, and to be sensitive to the ethical issues of modern work."

Advancing the quality and diversity of the workforce nationally and locally in her hometown of Chicago was a priority for Pritzker well before her term as commerce secretary. Beginning in 2012, Pritzker worked with other Chicago business leaders and personally provided seed funding to establish Skills for Chicagoland's Future, which works on "creating opportunities to increase economic mobility for Chicagoland area residents and solving talent solutions." The organization does this work not only by developing better training opportunities in collaboration with more than one hundred social-service organizations, but also by helping participants—who are mostly drawn from the long-term unemployed—to improve their interviewing skills for jobs, giving them better human work tools to navigate the complex systems for jobs and work. To date, the organization has helped thousands of job seekers by measurably advancing their "skills ROI." One concrete indicator of this ROI is that participants have experienced average annual income increases greater than $6,000.

When Pritzker arrived in Washington to work in the administration of her longtime friend Barack Obama, she immediately set out to meet with hundreds of business leaders and hear their concerns about trade and investment issues. But what she heard, as much as concerns about trade and taxes, was similar to what she had experienced in her own career as a business leader and philanthropic investor—anxiety about finding enough knowledgeable, skilled people to drive business success and national economic growth.

"When I went out early in my days at Commerce, workforce was consistently a top-three issue for every company we talked to, large and small," Pritzker said. "Business leaders would tell me, 'I can't find the talent I need for the kind of work we are doing today.'" At Commerce, Secretary Pritzker set out to do something that had never been done before by her predecessors: build a modern workforce development strategy well aligned with the department's historic focus on trade and economic growth.

The current system "doesn't provide the talent we need to support the needs of workers or the economic and social needs of the communities where they work," Pritzker noted. "I fundamentally believe the system that we have today doesn't work for either the workers or the employers. It's fixable, but it's going to require educators, business leaders, and labor to come together and actually work side by side on the solutions. I don't believe any one of those constituents can solve the problem on their own. The bottom line is that we need significant systems change to help more Americans adapt and thrive to create more inclusive prosperity."

At the conclusion of Obama's second term in early 2017, Pritzker returned to Chicago with a renewed enthusiasm for the task of building the new human work skills of today's workforce. She's especially focused on creating greater opportunities to advance human work skills in the digital economy with a large business collaborative called P33—a nod to the 1933 Chicago World's Fair. The initiative aims to regain by 2033 the city's stature as a center of innovation and human progress, much as the 1933 World's Fair did following the devastation of the Great Chicago Fire more than six decades earlier.

Because Chicago has the second-highest concentration of computer science graduates in the United States, Pritzker believes that the city could become a "Tier 1 tech hub" that taps the city's concentration of world-class universities, a diverse business base, an array of business incubators and accelerators, and workers motivated to not just earn money, but thrive.

"P33 can take us from a city that frankly has been punching below its weight class when it comes to the digital economy to the top tier by investing in the broad skills of our tech-focused workers," Pritzker said. "It's the key to getting them here, to keeping them here, and to the economic and social future of our community."

About Pathways, Life, and Human Work

We view education and work in linear terms—the time-honored School-College-Work pathway. But, of course, that's not the way life works, and the pathways we follow through it are seldom, if ever, linear. I was reminded of this when I heard the story of Herman Felton Jr., the president of Wiley College in Marshall, Texas. The display on the wall of his office reminds him and his visitors how far he has come from his humble beginnings. The only academic record hanging in his office, it is a collage of transcripts from the three Florida high schools he attended without earning a diploma.

"A lot of folks are afraid of where you start, but I embrace from whence we came and where we started," he said. Although he now holds bachelor's, law, and doctoral degrees, Felton, who is in his late 40s, said the transcripts of his indifferent early years in school remind him of the power of education to lift people from even the most modest circumstances.

"I grew up in a concrete jungle" in Jacksonville, Florida, he said. "My early aspirations were to be like drug dealers or the guys who left to play basketball or football or baseball at some junior college and then, most were away for just a year. I didn't think past high school and couldn't see past the nonsense I was doing." With six children, Felton's mother was "pretty much on her own" by the time she was 27, working two janitorial jobs six days a week to support the family, who lived in a housing project called Pottsburg Park. At the different high schools Felton attended, his transcripts record the grim details: a 1.29 grade point average, a class ranking of 425 out of 486, being held back in the 10th grade, and a slew of D's and F's in courses such as biology, English, history, and math.

Ten days after he turned 18, without a high school diploma, he enlisted in the U.S. Marines. As part of that commitment, he needed to complete his GED within a year. While preparing for that, he told an instructor that he had trouble reading. The instructor quickly recognized that Felton was dyslexic. "I had been afraid to say I had difficulty with reading," Felton said. "I'm disappointed now that I didn't have the nerve to admit it." But once the problem was diagnosed, and with some remedial help, Felton said that his "world changed from that day forward. It was a liberation." He finished his GED and spent eight years in the Marines.

During that time, he often did volunteer work in communities where he served. While working with a Big Brothers and Big Sisters program, he became friends with people who had been to college but seemed for him "to crush the myth that you had to be smart to go to college. They showed me I could go get a degree." After leaving military service, he needed a job. He worked at a car dealership, a collection agency, and the U.S. Postal Service, in a bulk mail sorting facility. That last job required long hours, work Felton said could easily be done now with robotics. One day, leaving work, he saw a young man in nice clothes driving a BMW. Felton asked what he did, and the man told him he worked in logistics, a job that required a college degree. That's when Felton realized he needed to go to college.

With his poor high school record, Felton was rejected by two colleges before Edward Waters College in Jacksonville admitted him under an open-door admissions policy. He graduated in three years with a bachelor's degree in political science and served as president of the Student Government Association. He wasn't sure what he would do next. A moment of serendipity changed things. One of his friends was headed to Gainesville from Jacksonville to interview at the University of Florida law school when his car broke down. He called Felton, who went to pick up his friend and drive him the rest of the way to Gainesville. Once there, the interviewer told Felton he might as well go through the process, too. He did and gained admission to the school. His friend didn't. "I had never had the desire to go to law school, but the doors a legal education opened to me were phenomenal," he said. "It really helped me develop my writing and thinking skills."

Just out of law school, he began his career in higher education, teaching a course and working in the development office at Murray State University in Kentucky. Three years later, Jimmy Jenkins, Felton's undergraduate president from Edward Waters, recruited Felton to join him at his new job at Livingstone College in North Carolina. He started at Livingstone as the president's executive assistant. During his nine years there, Felton was promoted through the administration's ranks to vice president and eventually senior vice president. While at Livingstone, "I knew I wanted to be a college president," Felton said.

In 2016, he got that opportunity when he was hired to become president of Wilberforce University in Ohio, the first private historically black college to be owned by African Americans. Two years later, when another mentor, Haywood Strickland, retired from Wiley, Felton was appointed to be his successor at the small private historically black college affiliated with the United Methodist Church.

Even as a college president, Felton has continued his education. He completed his Ph.D. in executive leadership from Jackson State in 2018, and has begun work toward a master's in theology from Southern Methodist University.

His experiences in life are reflected in his approach to the work of leading a college. During his first year at Wiley, he noticed that many students stayed on campus for Thanksgiving. Asked why, they told him that they couldn't afford to go home at Thanksgiving, return for the last few weeks of the semester, and then return home for Christmas. So, he convinced his board to change the fall calendar so that classes concluded before Thanksgiving. He's also convinced the board to reduce tuition from $21,000 per year to $17,500. At that level, Wiley students, 94% of whom qualify for federal Pell Grants, will be able to cover almost all the cost of their education using federal and state assistance.

Given his halting start in his own education, Felton finds it amazing that he now runs a university. "Never, ever, in my wildest dreams did I think I would get to be a college president, let alone two times," he said. "I've had some really good breaks and people who believed in me. But I have to admit, I'm astonished."

Felton will be the first one to say that he was lucky. But luck isn't a strategy. His story hints at how much undiscovered talent might be all around us, just looking for an opportunity to reveal itself. Building a learning system that nurtures and develops talent wherever it may live is our challenge—and our opportunity.

Herman Felton embodies the power of higher education to change people's lives, but his surprising journey also shows us why it doesn't work for so many people. Nothing in his background as a high school dropout predicted he would be able to even make it to college, much less succeed at the level he has. It was a GED instructor who discovered his learning disability. Even after serving in the military, he didn't believe higher education was for him, so he worked in dead-end jobs. But eventually, he broke through, and a world of opportunity opened up. Of course, it's also important that Felton's experience of life is what he draws on to do what has become his life's work. I find it revealing that Felton chose to work in a historically black college and is using his position to attack the systemic barriers that hold so many students back. I'm not sure that the solution to the problem of how to build the learning systems we so desperately need to prepare millions for human work is to find a couple thousand more Herman Feltons—I'm not sure they even exist. But we do need leaders who understand the main role of higher education is to help all students succeed throughout their lives.

The work of the future is difficult to predict, and even more difficult to pinpoint in terms of its potential disruption of both work and learning. But we do know this—preparing for the work of the future is essential, and it will require continuous improvement and constant attention over the lifetimes of those who hope to learn, earn, and serve others and those who will help them succeed in that human work.

Credentials for Human Work

"We'd all like to be certain of what we know, but I think the most important question is to ask yourself, do you really know what you know?"

—Marlon Brando[1]

A college graduate and a skilled musician, Majd Sekkar knew he needed to flee Syria, his home country, as its civil war raged. "I didn't see any future staying in my country," he said. "The future was dark." He originally thought he would move to Germany, but news reports of accidents involving boats crammed with immigrants scared him. After consulting with friends and some family members who had fled Syria for the United States in the 1980s, Sekkar decided to move to Canada because it "had opened the doors for Syrian refugees."

Sekkar and his sister arrived in Toronto in October 2016. Sekkar quickly found work in a restaurant, and, twenty days after his arrival, he was hired as a clarinet player with the Canadian Arabic Orchestra. He had graduated from the University of Aleppo in 2014 with a degree in finance and banking. Yet when he decided he wanted to pursue a degree in music in Canada, Humber College required a report that would provide an equivalency statement comparing the credential Sekkar had earned in Syria with a similar credential in Canada.

Obtaining official documents directly from his alma mater in Syria proved impossible, because Aleppo was the target of some of the civil war's most intense bombing campaigns. Then, Sekkar discovered the Centre for Immigration and Community Services, where he learned about the WES Gateway Program, designed for immigrants who have been forcibly displaced and lack academic documents. Having developed a way to evaluate and document the education background of Sekkar and other refugees who don't have access to original records, WES Gateway issued a credential evaluation report that would enable Sekkar to enter a bachelor's program.

In April 2018, Sekkar completed an eight-month certificate program, Introduction to Commercial Jazz Music, at Humber. With his WES evaluation and Humber certificate, Sekkar was accepted to Humber's bachelor's of music program without questions.

"Without the WES Gateway Program, I would not have been accepted to Humber College because I don't have a Canadian high school diploma, and I needed to get my academic credentials evaluated," Sekkar said.

Now in his late 20s, Sekkar is doing what he loves: studying music, teaching music, playing music. And he's learning two languages: English and jazz. "Jazz is like a new language for me," he said. "I had never played jazz before last September. And I love it, because you can mix any kind of music with jazz."

Remembering darker days in his home country and bleak days in office jobs, Sekkar said he feels "newborn" in his life in Canada. He plans to apply soon for Canadian citizenship and pursue his dream as a professional musician. "You can't be creative at something you don't like," he said. "I should enjoy my life and try to achieve my dream. I can pay my bills doing anything, but I want to be happy."

Most of us take our credentials for granted: if people are college graduates, they list the degree on a résumé and that's pretty much it. We assume that the major tells prospective employers, or anyone else, more or less what we know and can do. We assume the name of the college or university tells them what they need to know about the quality of our education. If someone wants proof that we really earned the credential, we have the institution send them our transcripts, and that's the end of the discussion.

But Sekkar's story reveals a darker truth behind many credentials. Too often, their value lies in a set of assumptions that are far from transparent and may not even be justified. What if employers have never heard of the institution or don't have firsthand experience with its graduates? Résumés may end up in the circular file, and applicants would never know why. What if they are immigrants or refugees and their credentials don't mean much to people in their new countries? They might never get opportunities to practice their professions, build on their educations, or start new lives.

The New World of Credentials

In an economy based on human work, developing knowledge and skills is essential, but it's not enough. For workers to have the chance at a good job and to advance in their careers, they need to understand the knowledge and skills they will need. For employers to find the people who can perform well in their jobs, they need to know the specific knowledge and skills their jobs require. Employers also need to know what the people they are thinking of hiring, or have hired, know and can do. Perhaps most important, workers also need to know what they know and can do so they can take advantage of whatever opportunities are available to them to build a satisfying career.

Credentials are how we document the knowledge and skills that jobs require and that people have. Many people around the world have them. A college degree is a credential to the extent that many jobs require one and people believe their degree indicates something important about what they know and can do.

Those with college degrees often have other kinds of credentials, too. Some individuals have industry-recognized certifications that carry great weight for getting good jobs and careers. In the United States, licenses issued by states are necessary to even work in many fields as diverse as law, medicine, nursing, and cosmetology. In some fields, having the credential of a Six Sigma black belt or Microsoft Certified Solutions Expert is a big deal. Credentials range from the most basic to the most advanced—both the Red Cross lifeguard certification and the board certification in emergency medicine represent mastery of valuable knowledge and skills that can lead to good jobs—whether a summer job at the local swimming pool for a high school student, or a position as a physician in a regional trauma center.

Most obviously, credentials represent mastery of bodies of knowledge and skills that can help people get good jobs and advance in their careers. But the power of credentials doesn't stop there. Employers use credentials to make the knowledge and skill requirements of their jobs clear to those who seek or hold them. That means that hiring managers can use the learning requirements for credentials to organize their education and training systems. Credentials also help people map out both career and learning pathways that will advance them throughout their lives. Today, someone can use credentials to map out a full career in nursing—from certified nursing assistant to licensed practical nurse to registered nurse to nurse practitioner—from a nondegree certificate all the way to a doctorate.

IT may be the field where the range of credentials is most dizzying—Google Certified Professional Cloud Architect,[2] Certified ScrumMaster,[3] and Certified Ethical Hacker[4] are all listed among the most in-demand and highest-paying credentials in the industry. Eighty-five percent of IT professionals have at least one certification, and many have several. Perhaps most revealing is that 66% of global IT professionals are already pursuing or plan to pursue their next certification—proving how continuous learning is integral to work in that field.[5] Given how central knowledge and skills are in a world of human work, we can expect other fields to look a lot more like IT when it comes to credentials, career ladders, and continuous learning.

But as it happens, the greatest strengths of today's systems for awarding credentials—their incredible diversity and flexibility—are also their greatest weaknesses. The strength of credentials, at least those based on a clear understanding of knowledge and skills, is that those who need to know what they mean, know what they mean. When an industry group defines the knowledge and skill requirements of an occupation, people who want to work in that industry can have a clear idea of what credentials they need to move up the ladder. Education and training providers can design programs to teach the knowledge and skills required for the credential. Employers can focus their talent searches on people who can do the job. So far, so good.

But what happens to people who have credentials in one field and now want to work in another? They have no way to know how the knowledge and skills their credentials represent align with those of a different credential in another field. What about someone who has gained significant knowledge and skills through work, military service, or education in one country but doesn't know how those credentials might help in another country? There is usually no way to apply learning from one field to a credential in another.

What about the millions of people who don't have a credential at all? They don't even know where to start to get a credential that might qualify them for good jobs. As we have already seen, vast numbers of people now need more advanced learning—in fact, we should be working toward a system in which everyone learns at a level that until now has been considered college level. School, the first step on our current talent pathway, may have done a decent job preparing people for work when most jobs were based on repetitive tasks, but it is wholly inadequate for human work.

Let's be honest. When it comes to contemporary life in the United States, other than providing a good excuse for a ceremony and a party, a high school diploma is frighteningly inadequate as a credential today. It signifies little in terms of readiness for either work or further education, and it doesn't improve the quality of life of most people in measurable ways. In fact, we may think about the radical idea of abolishing the high school diploma and replacing it with credentials of actual value in today's economy—such as an associate degree or industry-recognized certification—and make sure that everyone has the opportunity to earn them.

And what about people with college degrees? It's true that they have a credential of some value in the job market, but they usually don't really know what they can do with it, and neither do employers. Sadly, college graduates often find out that there is at best an imperfect fit between what they have studied and what they need to do to take advantage of the opportunities for work that may exist for them. But there is an even deeper problem. For most graduates of higher education, it is not clear what they have learned—in other words, no one can tell what they know and can do.

While some people question whether students learn much of anything in college,[6] that's not the problem here. Even when students learn everything that their professors hope for, not being able to describe what they know and can do in ways that they and employers can understand is a huge problem. That's not all—everyone needs to keep learning and developing talent, and not knowing what one already has learned makes it difficult, if not impossible, to identify pathways to further learning.

The basic problem with our current approach to credentials is its lack of transparency. By transparency, I am talking specifically about three big problems that we need to overcome to be prepared for a world of human work.

Problem 1: It's not clear what most credentials represent in terms of knowledge, skills, and abilities.

Credentials represent learning that people have acquired—in the form of knowledge, skills, and abilities—and therefore serve as the interface between learning and work. There is an extraordinary array of them. Nearly 740,000 unique credentials are issued by colleges, workforce agencies, licensing entities, and other credential issuers in the United States alone.[7] Most, but not all, credentials have value in the labor market because they represent the ability to do something of value to employers.

But there is a profound lack of transparency about what those credentials represent. Even when people know that a certain credential is useful or necessary to get a certain job, they may not know what it takes to get it, what it represents in terms of knowledge and skills, what kind of career pathways it opens up, or how it relates to other credentials. Fixing this may seem a tall order, but we do know how to do it. The key is for credentials to represent not the kind of experience individuals have had, educational or otherwise, but the knowledge and skills they have obtained—in other words, their learning.

As valuable as knowledge and skills are, it's not enough just to assure that people have the opportunity to learn what they need. For a future of human work, that learning must be made clear, transparent, and recognized. Only by making people's learning transparent can an economy based on knowledge and skills really work, giving people the fullest opportunity to apply what they know and can do.

Problem 2: Employers, educators, and individuals all speak different languages when it comes to knowledge and skills.

The basic terms everyone uses to describe knowledge, skills, and abilities are the same, but the meaning attached to them is left wide open for interpretation. For example, employers consistently identify higher-level thinking skills such as problem solving and an ability to work in a team as the ones they most desire in employees, and they also consistently report difficulty finding people with them.[8] But educators believe they are doing a good job developing these same skills. The discrepancy in perceptions is sizable: while 96% of chief academic officers believe their colleges or universities do a good job preparing graduates, only 11% of business leaders say higher education is producing graduates with the specific skills and competencies their businesses need.[9]

Individuals, whether as students or workers, don't know what to believe. Part of the problem is that terms such as "problem solving" and "ability to work in a team" don't really say much about what the specific skill is that employers are looking for or that educators are teaching.

This is a particular problem with college degrees. People accept that a college degree holder has learned *something* of value, but they usually don't know exactly what that something is. From experience, employers may know that people who hold a particular degree from a particular institution can perform well in a particular job, but when presented with a degree they are not familiar with, they often don't know what to make of it.

An even bigger problem is that people who hold a degree often don't know what it means, either. Of course, they know they have a degree in a particular major, and they may even know that it generally qualifies them for certain jobs. But they may not actually know what they know and can do—at least, not clearly enough to communicate it to potential employers. Aside from making it harder than it needs to be to find a job they're qualified for—and for employers to find them—it makes it hard for them to know what else they can do if they want or need to change careers. Nondegree credentials are a bit better in this regard because they tend to be tied to particular occupations, but they become almost meaningless when individuals try to move their careers in new directions.

In contrast, transparent credentials make clear what they mean in terms of learning to everyone who uses them—learners and workers, certainly, but also education providers and employers.

Problem 3: Pathways through education and careers are either nonexistent or nearly impossible for outsiders to fathom.

Let's consider how a typical learner—I'll call her Shyvon—navigates today's education systems and the labor market. To get a good job after high school, Shyvon realizes that she needs a credential of value. What she has learned from her high school counselor, her family and friends, and the media is that this usually means a college degree. Shyvon has learned from these sources that the pathways to get one are based on their components—courses and credits.

Shyvon can easily grasp the math behind what it takes to move through the system by accumulating credits and then a degree, which offers standing for the next step on the pathway. Sixty credits lead to an associate degree, 120 lead to a bachelor's, a bachelor's leads to a master's, and so on. This system is so ingrained that it's hard to imagine that it could be questioned or that anything could replace it. But there are a lot of problems with this system for Shyvon and learners like her. And in a world of human work, those problems are getting worse.

For one thing, today's credentials system has a lot of trouble considering any learning that did not take place in a traditional college setting for credit. Even today, hundreds of thousands of veterans have trouble getting recognition for the knowledge and skills—and credentials—that they earned through their military service. We offer those veterans a few choices, none of which work very well: they can hope to get credit for their learning after a long process of prior learning assessment (one that is not widely available), they can attend an institution of questionable reputation that will give them credit for their experience, or they can start over and take courses that teach them things they already know. Whichever route they take, the message to our vets is unmistakable: you don't really belong here.

But let's say they obtain a college degree or other credential and are now ready to start a career. It seems simple enough—they find jobs they believe they'd like and are qualified for, apply and submit résumés and reference letters, and have interviews in which they answer questions potential employers have about their ability to perform. Of course, this isn't the way it works in the real world. For one thing, it's hard for them to know whether they're qualified for the jobs because the job descriptions include vague statements (such as "effective problem solver") without definitions. For another, they really have no idea whether employers believe the institutions they've attended, degrees they've earned, and work experiences they've collected match up with what employers are looking for. The interviews, if they're lucky enough to get them, generally serve to confirm what they already suspected, which is that the process is highly subjective and impossible to understand from the outside.

What happens when former employers have gone out of business or jobs have been eliminated and they need to change jobs—perhaps to jobs in different industries? Maybe they have credentials that mattered in their prior jobs and people there knew what they meant, but that may not help them now. People with industry-recognized certifications in a skilled trade may have a range of analytical and problem-solving skills gained through both education and training and real-world experience. These skills are highly relevant in a range of settings, and it should be possible to build on them when workers need to go in new directions.

As occupations and industries are disrupted—with jobs lost and gained in unpredictable ways—giving people the tools to move into a new field without having to relearn something they already know is crucial. Transparency about the meaning of credentials in terms of learning would finally lead to a system in which all learning counts wherever, whenever, and however it is obtained, and all this learning can be used to build pathways through rewarding careers.

Of course, employers have all these same problems from the other side. They don't know what candidates actually know and can do, so they look for people who "fit the profile" of people who have performed adequately in the past, even if that means they keep looking at people from the same institutions and keep hiring people who look the same, often literally, as the ones they've hired before. The result, as shown clearly in the data, is employers can't find enough people with the knowledge and skills they need, and people who could do the job—or learn how to do it if given the chance—don't get the opportunity they so desperately seek.

Making Credentials Transparent

Transparent credentials make the relationship between them, in terms of knowledge and skills, clear to all. This applies whether we are talking about credentials in a particular field or across fields. In the first case, knowing the relationship between credentials in, say, manufacturing, would allow people to map out career pathways in terms of knowledge and skills—a learning pathway—rather than just through jobs. Rather than wonder how to advance in their careers, people would know what they need to learn to move to better opportunities. Of course, employers also would be well served by making this knowledge widely available.

At first glance, it seems impossible to make credentials truly transparent. There are so many of them—740,000 is an almost unfathomable number. There are numerous kinds, from certificates and certifications to diplomas and degrees. Credentials are awarded at multiple levels, from those offered after weekend training courses to those requiring years of study after people earn bachelor's degrees. They are issued by thousands of institutions and organizations, from colleges and universities to corporate or industry-based training programs.

What does it mean to make credentials transparent? The first step is to use common frameworks to define knowledge and skills. Frameworks define skills in terms specific and clear enough to get everyone on the same page. There are lots of skill frameworks in use, especially around technical skills in particular industries. They start at a high level, such as problem solving, but then drill down to define the specific competencies people need to develop to master each skill. By defining competencies, frameworks add something critical to the discussion—a clear understanding of what a skill looks like in practice so that everyone can know whether a person has it or not.

But the real power of common frameworks emerges when they are used to organize comprehensive learning systems and with labor markets at a national level. Creating a national skill framework may seem like a tall order for a country as big and diverse as the United States. But national skill frameworks are the norm, not the exception, in most of the rest of the developed world. Countries as diverse as the United Kingdom, South Africa, Australia, New Zealand, and Japan all have national skill frameworks and rely on them to align education and employment.

The European Qualifications Framework (EQF) was developed by the European Commission to make credentials comparable across all EU member countries. Imagine the difficulty of aligning credentials across such a diverse range of national educational systems, languages, and employment markets. And yet, skills frameworks such as the EQF make this possible. The EQF is even used to integrate private-sector qualifications into national qualification systems and is helping to validate informal learning outside of the education system.[10]

When it comes to using frameworks to define knowledge and skills, the United States is the outlier. America never bothered to develop a national skills framework, probably because our systems are so decentralized that no one could really take the lead. Our decentralized systems offer a lot of advantages, but we should acknowledge that it slows our ability to respond to pressing national needs. This is a good example of where a concerted effort to bring the various players together—universities, community colleges, employers, workforce development systems, unions, industry groups—would really pay off.

Because the development and use of frameworks is limited in the United States, most of the learning that is taking place here—and there is a lot of it—is haphazard. Employers, educators, and individuals themselves do not know what they have or what it means. As a result, for a lot of people, it doesn't add up to the kind of recognized learning that leads to a better job or more fulfilling work.

But frameworks alone are not the answer: using a common framework to build a transparent system is. Again, this sounds like a tall order, but we now take transparency for granted in numerous other fields in which the challenges are similar. We can book hotels and flights online anywhere in the world after comparing prices and features using common definitions. We can access our financial information in much the same way despite the numerous, highly competitive companies that control it. We can research and compare almost any product or service by perusing aggregated online reviews and comments after sorting them based on the criteria important to us.

All this is possible because the massive amount of information underlying these systems relies on a common framework—a descriptive language—that allows for the construction of online tools to freely access all of it. It's an amazing transformation of how we use information, even more so because it's all so simple and seamless that users are scarcely aware of the complexity.

Credential Engine, a U.S.-based not-for-profit organization established in 2017, is using just such a language for credentials, called the Credential Transparency Descriptive Language (CTDL). This language, conceived by researchers a few years before Credential Engine was formed, is essentially a web-based protocol, like the more commonly known HTML. It allows different computers, platforms, and systems to speak the same language about credentials. With this new online language, Credential Engine is developing a powerful new tool called a Credential Registry with the capability to sort and arrange up-to-date information about all credentials, including what each represents in terms of learning skills, who awards it, and how the credential can be used.

But this is not the true point of what Credential Engine is building. The CTDL and registry constitute a platform upon which multiple new applications can be built to allow anyone to search and retrieve information about credentials. This is, in effect, the DNA of a new system of transparent credentials, one in which learning can be linked to knowledge, skills, and abilities through credentials and in which employers, consumers, and credential issuers can all connect in much more transparent and authentic ways than are possible through existing platforms. Apps could emerge for people looking for credentials that lead to good jobs, or for employers wanting to know which credentials represent the knowledge and skills they are looking for, or for people to design learning programs that develop the skills people need.

None of this is being done by government at any level. The travel site Orbitz was developed by a consortium of airlines themselves, each one in fierce competition with the others. Likewise, the infrastructure for credential transparency will be built by the participants in the system out of collective self-interest. Transparent credentials should provide benefits to individuals and providers alike, and once the system reaches critical mass, it should become virtually all-inclusive.

Transparency around learning can change credentials in fundamental ways. For the work of the future, credentials won't be a piece of paper framed and hung on a wall. A credential can be anything that represents real learning—anything that demonstrates a competency or mastery of a set of skills. It could be a degree or recognized certification, but it could also be the result of an assessment, including one based on examples of prior work. Entirely new kinds of credentials will doubtless emerge. But when credentials are based on common definitions and standards, what they all mean and how they relate to each other will be clear.

With transparent credentials, everyone will be able to build a personal profile, essentially a learning passport, showing what they know and can do. While these learning passports may have a superficial resemblance to a portfolio, they will be far richer because of their transparency regarding the knowledge and skills they represent. Transparent credentials will make it possible for people to use their talent, regardless of what they bring to the table or what kind of job they do.

A great example of this idea in action is the European Union initiative called Europass.[11] While Europass includes several components, the most important are a standard CV (or résumé) template, available in twenty-nine languages, and a European Skills Passport that people can create and attach to their CV to document their skills and qualifications. The scale of Europass is impressive. More than 22 million Europass CVs were created online in 2018, and about 130 million in total since 2005. More than 2.4 million CVs had been created online as of January 2019, which is up 17% compared with January 2018. At this scale, it should be obvious that making credentials transparent is hardly a sideshow or "interesting" concept—it is both necessary and possible.

Making credentials transparent by using common frameworks and languages to build recognition systems even stronger than Europass is a big deal. Directly, it would allow literally millions of people to better leverage their knowledge and skills in an economy based on human work. Indirectly, its effect may be even greater by allowing us to create flexible, competency-based pathways through learning and careers.

Transparent credentials are based on the actual knowledge and skills—the competencies—a person has gained rather than where they went to school or how long they spent studying something. By the same token, pathways through learning shouldn't be based on accumulating credits through time spent in a classroom, hopefully with learning as a byproduct. Instead, pathways should be based solely on the specific knowledge and skills people gain through formal education, work, informal learning, or simply through life experience. Today, competency-based learning is an alternative, a sideline, an interesting experiment. But that's not the way it should be. I'm not exaggerating when I say *all* education should be competency-based because it's a better way to organize learning.

Competency-Based Learning

Competency-based pathways look different. Consider the case of Jamie Dear, who was looking for a bachelor's program that would allow him to upgrade his associate degree in business. He found the Flex program at the University of Wisconsin—a self-paced competency-based approach built around direct assessment and projects rather than fixed schedules and seat time. In ten months, rather than the several years it typically takes working students to complete a degree, he earned a bachelor's in information science and technology, which led to Google and one of their prestigious and highly selective training programs. Google selected Dear not just because the company could see exactly what content and technical skills he had mastered—in large part by looking at the projects he had done—but also because Google recognized the self-discipline required to complete a competency-based degree through UW Flex.[12]

Competency-based pathways through learning and jobs will become the norm and not the exception. A good example of how this may look at scale can be found in Singapore. Through a national initiative called SkillsFuture Singapore, the country is using its national skills framework to create more flexible pathways for individuals through both education and employment. The intention is that no one hits a dead end, and SkillsFuture is assuring this by guaranteeing that pathways exist from all levels of the education system—vocational, technical, and academic—through all of Singapore's industries and employers. To back this system up and encourage people to improve their skills, every Singaporean 25 and older receives a SkillsFuture Credit—$500 initially, with periodic top-ups—with the express goal for people to "take ownership of their skills development and lifelong learning."[13]

The Singapore experience points to another important development: the creation of competency-based pathways based on shorter-term, stackable credentials. There are a lot of reasons to move in this direction. Careers today are seldom linear—they look less like a ladder than a climbing wall, where the way to

move up may involve moving sideways or even down to get a
better hold on a route forward. Likewise, learning something—
whether it's knowledge or a skill—opens many possible routes to
further learning. These flexible, dynamic pathways are best supported by credentials that reflect "modules" of learning. We're
seeing a dizzying array of these credentials emerge, including digital badges and an explosion of competency-based certifications.[14]
Some providers are even trying to stake a claim to the terms
used to describe these new credentials. "Nanodegree," "Micro-
Bachelors," and even "MicroDegree" are registered trademarks
of three different providers.[15]

Once again, some countries are taking the lead in leveraging
these innovations. For many years, Australia has had a robust
learning framework, the Australian Qualifications Framework,
that is widely used by employers, colleges and universities, training providers, and government to align their efforts to develop
knowledge and skills. Australia is now in the process of using the
AQF to include shorter-term credentials into its comprehensive
national system.[16]

Our current systems won't work in the future. They barely
work now. We desperately need a more open and transparent
way to navigate learning and careers, and we have the building
blocks to create it. Common language about skills will allow
people to know what they need to know and be able to do at
each stage of their learning journeys and at each stage of their
careers, and transparent credentials will allow them to show
they're ready for the next steps—both educationally and in terms
of careers. Pathways will be built around knowledge and skills—
in other words, learning—rather than guesses and reputations.

Obviously, all this means big changes for education—especially higher education. Nearly our entire system of higher
education is based on the belief that quality is intrinsic to the institution rather than the learning that students obtain. Everything
from how many applicants universities get, how much they can
charge students and families, what kind of faculty they can draw,
and especially how much money they can raise is a function of

perceptions of quality based on what rankers and researchers call "reputational" factors.

Of course, this idea of quality goes hand in glove with an elitist system in which colleges and universities operate as gatekeepers. Today, it's clear this system is breaking down, and not just because a few B-list celebrities got caught paying off college functionaries to game the system for their children.

Today, with more and better information about learning and credentials, consumers are gaining greater leverage in the marketplace. As we've seen in other industries, such as the travel industry, consumers' ability to navigate the system means that pressure will be on the established brands to produce results that consumers want. These brands won't be able to say, "Trust us, we know best" about what learners need. The British megafirm Thomas Cook failed after nearly 200 years as a travel icon because consumers ultimately decided that they wanted more than the simplicity and peace of mind that came from relying on an old-line travel agency. They wanted better options, lower prices, and a more self-defined experience. And they got that from Expedia, Orbitz, and other aggregators. A reduction in brand power in higher education because of better information means that the system overall will be better, because it will ultimately rest on what people know and can do with their credentials.

The Need for Higher and Wider *Learning*

Let's return to the notion of wide learning. Wide learning—the idea that we need to view the learning dimensions of human work as including a wide range of time, people, and content—is different from what we today call higher education. But, for the record, this is not a call to eliminate higher education. Far from it. Wide learning includes broad, integrative thinking skills such as problem solving and abstract reasoning, and it also includes advanced technical skills that are constantly changing and evolving. In addition, wide learning includes attributes such as caring and empathy that also are learned, but through experiences that we need to assure people can have.

Anne-Marie Slaughter, chief executive of New America, is a foreign policy expert and award-winning author of numerous books on global security as well as gender issues. Slaughter talks of the importance of caring when it comes to developing learners, and to the work those learners will do over the course of their lifetimes. In 2016, she spoke at the commencement for the University of Utah and told graduates that they should always make room "for the precious, indispensable, and priceless work of care."

"In the industrial economy, we hired hands. In the knowledge economy, we hire heads. In the human economy, we will hire hearts," Slaughter told the assembled graduates. "Machines will be increasingly intelligent and, indeed, for those who are in computing science, you know those machines will learn in very much the same way that humans learn. What humans will bring are the traits of our heart—the traits that cannot be programmed into software."[17]

Slaughter's observations about caring and empathy as key human traits are important, as is her perspective that these traits must be nurtured and continually developed. Colleges and universities are extremely important as places where this kind of learning can take place. But they are not the only places where learning can and does happen, and they are not the sole arbiters of who is qualified to move ahead in the world. Transparent credentials will open doors of opportunity to people regardless of where or how they developed their knowledge and skills.

This is not a semantic exercise. Focusing on learning takes us in a different—and ultimately more constructive—direction. A focus on wider learning causes us to ask important questions about the broad knowledge and skills that people need to meet the demands for talent in our communities and nations. We must work on assuring that this learning—wherever and however it is obtained—is recognized by transparent credentials that communicate knowledge and skills to employers, education providers, and the individuals who hold the credentials. In short, we need to prepare people for whatever comes in an uncertain world and help people to keep learning throughout their lives as the world changes around them.

The most important reason for making credentials transparent and clear is that people themselves need to know what they know and can do. In today's economy, and even more in tomorrow's, people need to own their learning in much the same way as they need to own their health. People's ability to advance—to get better jobs and do more fulfilling work—depends on their talent, and to take advantage of it, they need to know what it is. Transparent credentials are owned by the people who earn them, and they make it possible for them to leverage their learning in whatever ways they can to advance their careers, do meaningful work, and build better lives for themselves and their families.

Focusing on knowledge and skills allows us to see learning and working as two sides of the same coin. Rather than learning *to* work, in a world of human work, learning *is* working, and working *is* learning.

The implications of this shift for our systems of education and employment—or more precisely, learning and earning—are profound. And it's the next logical step in the evolution of the human work ecosystem.

Earning and Learning

"I've learned that making a living is not the same thing as making a life."

—Maya Angelou[1]

At 21, with a 2-year-old son, Teresa Riggins Smith was unemployed and on public assistance. But she found out about the CVS Registered Apprenticeship Program, which the drugstore chain started to help fill the 70,000 pharmacy technician positions it believes it will need to hire to meet the growing demand for medication among aging baby boomers. In the early 2000s, CVS looked at the career paths of its often low-income, front-line, high school–educated retail employees and began a program, loosely modeled on programs in the skilled trades, to prepare many of them for careers as pharmacy technicians. Workers learn while they earn and gain a registered apprentice credential to advance their work prospects over the long term, including management positions in the company's nearly 10,000 retail stores.[2]

CVS has since extended the program to include workers displaced by realignment, site relocations, or technology. As of 2017, the company employed 4,600 apprenticeship-trained pharmacy technicians and management employees in twelve states. It's ironic that drugs are central to Smith's career and thus her future, because they certainly shaped her past. She and her siblings had spent much of their childhoods shuttling in and out of foster homes, collateral damage caused by their parents' drug abuse.

When she was 19, a year after graduating from high school, Smith had her first child and applied for public assistance. The system requires recipients to make good-faith efforts to support themselves and their families—a requirement that often leads to a series of dead-end, low-paying jobs. The cycle is indeed vicious. But it can be disrupted—as it was when Smith attended a presentation about the CVS apprenticeship program. "A lot of people weren't interested," Smith recalled. "But my eyes were glued on her. I listened to everything she had to say, because it was something I already wanted to do." Smith peppered the CVS Workforce Initiatives manager with questions about the application, the training, and the odds of landing a job—a prospect that, just hours earlier, had seemed hopelessly out of reach.

The path to a pharmacy tech position begins with a screening and an invitation to apply. Those accepted into the program undergo intense training to acquaint them with the dizzying array of medications a tech might handle on any given day and the intricacies of a job in which there is no room for error. Apprentices are paid an hourly salary during the four-week training period. Once training is complete, CVS places the candidates in stores for an eighty-hour externship that almost always leads to a formal job offer.

Teresa Smith's first day at CVS is one she'll never forget. "I was only making minimum wage, $7.50" an hour, she said. "But when I took this job, it felt as if I was walking into a six-figure salary." Her enthusiasm soon gained the attention of management and, within a year, Smith was promoted to shift supervisor. "I went in and learned everything I could," she said. Just three years after Smith began her apprenticeship, CVS tapped her to manage a location in suburban Highland Park, Michigan. Turns out she didn't just manage the pharmacy; she staved off a possible store closing by working to reorient employees and improve their overall performance. Smith insists she's only doing what comes naturally, whether it's nudging her employees to up their game or persuading young customers to follow her path.

"My goal is to bring people like me to CVS, train them, and help them to be a success," she said. "Success comes in many different boxes. It doesn't have to mean you're a millionaire. Success can be taking care of your family or making sure your gas and electric aren't cut off. I look for key qualities when I hire. I want to help, so I give them my background and I look for my passion."

Smith's story highlights the power of work to transform lives. It also shows how the traits that lead to success can be something that people don't normally learn in school—compassion, empathy, or the trait Teresa Smith has and looks for, passion. This points to what we need. Simply put, we need a system that integrates formal learning with the wide learning that human work requires however and wherever it happens. How do we create such a system? The answer is surprisingly easy. It's by focusing on learning rather than education, and on work rather than jobs.

The difference between learning and education is that the former is what the individual does, and the latter is what schools and colleges provide. Likewise, work is what the individual does, and jobs are what employers provide. The future of work—a future in which the uniqueness of humans is the driver—will require both the education and employment systems to change to focus on individuals. After all, the learner and the worker are the same person. Right now, the two systems focus on very different things, so it's only natural that they should be separate, use different languages, and have vastly different objectives. When they change to focus on the individual, the worker-learner, they become one.

The End of the School-College-Work Pathway

For more than a century, most people in the United States have proceeded on the same life path. First, they learn. Then, they work. As children and young adults, they go to school to get the basic knowledge we all need. From there, they should be able to enter the workforce unless they want more education to land better jobs, in which case they go to college. After that, they go to work. Through work, they gain experience and skills, which can lead to better jobs and successful careers. It's a well-understood, linear, and ingrained pathway—School, College, Work.

But in the face of the talent gap and the new challenge posed by human work, the School-College-Work pathway is breaking down. In one recent survey of senior business executives, 92% said that American workers are not as skilled as they need to be. Fifty-nine percent of them blamed our education systems for not doing more to address this challenge.[3] In fairness, the executives don't see business as blameless: 89% believe apprenticeship and better corporate training programs would help. But they cite the cost of the programs and lukewarm commitment by executive leadership, not lack of employee interest, as the main reason they do not expand to meet the need. These executives also see the skills gaps as being most severe in higher-level skills such as communication, creativity, critical thinking, and collaboration—not in technical or software skills. Once again, we see the need to develop higher-level skills in millions of people as the essence of the problem.

Most people working in the field of education know that the simple School-College-Work pathway stopped being the model for most people a long time ago. It was replaced with what educators have called lifelong learning—first people learn, then they work, then they learn some more, then apply it to their work, and repeat. But even in this model, we view learning as something people do in education systems and work as something they do in the employment system.

Frankly, "lifelong learning" also seems off-putting from the consumer perspective. It sounds more like a prison sentence than an opportunity. It's a process of stepping away from what people want to do, which is work, in order to build skills that are likely to expire. It's one reason the concept has largely remained in the realm of education policy analysts and is not how most people want to see themselves. Plus, I suspect for a lot of people, "lifelong learning" means a lifetime of paying for college—something that is, frankly, terrifying.

The divided notions of learning and working are breaking down in the world of human work. As we've seen, human work is different from the work that can be automated and done by machines. By its nature, human work relies on people's core abilities, nurtured and developed by gaining knowledge and skills through a wide range of life experiences, formal and informal education, and, certainly, through work. This combination of abilities, knowledge, and skills, which evolves throughout life, is what we should be calling "talent."

While developing talent has always been important to individual success, fostering and deploying talent on a large scale has become essential as the economy shifts to one based on human work. Think about this from the point of view of employers. In a talent-based economy, what employees know and can do is the bread and butter of the enterprise. Talent is the driver of success at all levels—individual, corporate, and national. What this means is that learning *is* the work, and the highest purpose of work is that it leads to learning.

In other words, work is learning, and learning is work. And they happen together in the human work ecosystem.

We have talked about how the emergence of talent as the key driver of the economy—and individual success within it—has serious implications for our education systems. But the implications of human work may call for even bigger changes on the part of employers. In the human work ecosystem, education and employment are tied together in unprecedented ways. Indeed, they are merging into one activity.

This integration begins with the knowledge that the School-College-Work pathway that we have come to know and expect is broken, and that there is no point trying to fix it. For starters, it doesn't do a very good job of preparing people for human work. People need the constantly changing technical skills in demand in the economy, but they also need strong foundational learning in higher-level thinking and a range of valuable skills and abilities that cut across all occupations—including communication, problem solving, empathy, and creativity. Human work demands that these different kinds of learning be integrated—they work together in the real world, and they need to be learned together.

That means we need a new kind of learning system that combines what we now view as education (for foundational learning) and training (for technical skills), not the two separate and distinct systems we are so accustomed to. Furthermore, work is the place where much of this learning takes place, and the learning is what gives value to the work. It's really an ecosystem where all these separate processes are integrated and mutually dependent.

Apprenticeships—New Relevance for an Old Idea

The fact that so many of today's students have jobs or are doing contractual work while in college is a clue about how to move away from the obsolete School-College-Work pathway. Although we continue to believe the "average" college student gets a job after graduating from college, the fact is that two-thirds are employed while in college, and four out of ten are employed full-time. A lot of students actually bring significant work experience to college with them—half of all students are financially independent of their parents, a third are over 25, and six out of one hundred have served or are serving in the armed forces.[4] The notion of students as "empty vessels" is seriously outdated.

Work offers many opportunities for learning, and yet in most cases it is kept separate from school and college education. At best, we consider it only as the endpoint of education—where people go when they're finished with education. Even when we consider higher education's role in addressing the need to update knowledge and skills through people's careers, we call it lifelong learning—the idea that people need to return to college from time to time before going back to work. This ping-pong approach to education and work is better than the once-and-done approach, but it still maintains the fiction that learning and working are separate activities in distinct systems operating under their own sets of rules.

An exception to this rule is apprenticeships, and interest in this ancient model is growing as a way to address our very modern challenges. Apprenticeships are used around the world, but models differ from country to country, as do the roles apprenticeships play in preparing people for work. In the United Kingdom, apprenticeships have accelerated in recent years thanks to a "levy" imposed on large employers to support a wide array of apprenticeship opportunities—at all types of employers, not just those that pay into the program. Companies pay the equivalent of 0.5% of their total payroll toward the apprenticeship program, providing resources for almost half of all apprenticeships in the United Kingdom. Between 2017 and 2019, the program helped more than 300,000 people begin their apprenticeships.[5]

In the United States, around a half-million people participate in apprenticeships of some type[6]—a significant number, but not as many in proportion to population as in other countries. In America, apprenticeships are most prevalent in the skilled trades, especially the building trades. The occupations with a sizable number of apprentices include carpenters, electricians, plumbers, and sheet-metal workers.

For many years, Germany and Switzerland were the models for how apprenticeship programs should work. In 2015, calculations indicated that more than half of all German workers (52.4%) entered the workforce through an apprenticeship, and 1.34 million people were in an apprenticeship—a much higher proportion of the workforce than in the United States.[7] As an integral part of Germany's dual education system, apprenticeships are the primary way individuals enter the workforce there, and indeed in many fields it is virtually impossible to do so without one.

But the apprenticeship models that hold the most promise for meeting the needs of the work of the future are those that blend resources from employers and education providers into a unified work-learn experience. Take for example the experience of Nicholas Kwiatkowski. He wasn't sure what he wanted to do after graduating from high school in Mount Holly, North Carolina, so he stayed at a job he had during high school, helping to manage an Italian restaurant. "I didn't think it was viable to go to school, waste money, pile up student debt and not know what I wanted to do," Kwiatkowski said.

But thanks to his younger brother, Lukas, Kwiatkowski found a new job and the path to an entirely new career at Blum Inc., a manufacturer of high-tech latches, hinges, and slide components for cabinetry. Lukas had signed up for the Apprenticeship 2000 program at Blum while attending East Gaston High School in Mount Holly. That's the normal entry point into the program, which works closely with Charlotte-area high schools to identify promising students for the apprenticeship program.

As Nicholas learned more about Blum and the apprenticeship program, he decided to apply for a job at Blum. He applied three times before finally landing a job as a press operator. He became a team leader within months of starting the job in May 2016, but he had higher aims. As a regular Blum employee, his prospects for advancement were limited. But if he could enter the Apprenticeship 2000 program, the promise for future promotions and higher pay was greater. After being employed at Blum for a year, he was able to apply for the program, which accepted him in 2017, a year after Lukas completed his apprenticeship.

Apprenticeship 2000 was started by Blum and other Charlotte-area companies in 1995. The program offers technical career opportunities to high school students and a few older students (Nicholas Kwiatkowski included). The program is extremely rare in the United States, requiring 8,000 hours of training and education for each apprentice, including 6,400 hours at

the companies that employ them and 1,600 hours of classes at
Central Piedmont Community College in Charlotte. Upon graduation, an apprentice receives an associate degree in mechatronics
engineering from the college and a journeyman's certificate from
the North Carolina Department of Commerce. "Our job is to
build the next strong workforce," said Andreas Thurner, the apprenticeship manager at Blum. "You can have the best equipment
in the world, but it's worthless if you don't have the right people
on it."[8]

Blum's financial commitment to the program is significant:
Thurner said the Austria-based company has $1.8 million in
equipment and three full-time instructors in the training area
of its Stanley, North Carolina, production facility. And each
apprentice represents a $175,000 commitment from Blum to
provide pay and benefits during the bachelor's program. The
screening process for applicants is intense. At any one time, Blum
has only about sixteen students in the program. Those who graduate are loyal to the company: Thurner estimates that 75% of
the graduates at Blum have stayed with the company five years
or more after graduating, even though they are not required to
stay under terms of the apprenticeship program.

"We guarantee you employment. We guarantee you a salary of
$36,000 at the end of the program," Thurner said. "Who does that?
Who pays for your college and then gives you a guaranteed job?"

For Nicholas Kwiatkowski, now in his mid-20s, the program
schedule is intense: he spends four ten-hour days at Blum and
goes to classes at Central Piedmont one afternoon per week.
After two years in the program, he and his trainers decided he
would be best suited to be a tool-and-die maker, the same role
his brother has at Blum. By 2021, he plans to have finished the
apprenticeship, earned a degree, and set a better course for his
future. "Honestly, I'm surprised not more companies do this,"
he said. "Hiring outside people with a degree is okay, but why
not invest in what you have? If you have employees who are
bright and can be trained, why not train them? I'm sure there are

tons of people out there who would like to have a chance to go through a program like this."

In other countries, programs such as the one Kwiatkowski went through are becoming the norm rather than the exception. The United Kingdom has developed and implemented a system of "higher and degree apprenticeships," which extend the apprenticeship model to many other fields in which they were not traditionally used. Rather than a singular focus on skilled trades, in the United Kingdom apprenticeships are available in fields as diverse as engineering, health care, financial services, social work, and the performing arts.[9]

One example of a degree apprenticeship in the United Kingdom is the product design and development engineer apprenticeship for the automobile industry. The engineers work on all the stages of creating modern automobiles and their component parts, which calls upon a wide range of skills. They must be able to develop concepts and designs, use computer-aided design (CAD) and rapid prototyping tools, and test and analyze performance. All of this is done as part of teams that include suppliers and managers. The apprenticeship begins with a foundation stage to develop core engineering skills, including both fundamental scientific and mathematical principles and hands-on experience such as producing electrical drawings and models, operating lathes and milling equipment, and using a wide range of computer software.

Crucially, this apprenticeship, and others in the United Kingdom, lead to a recognized credential—in this case, a bachelor's degree. As such, they combine both academic and technical learning, but unlike typical degree programs, these apprenticeships are designed by industry, and most learning takes place on the job. Yet the fact that they lead to a degree means they can never be a dead end. An individual who completes this kind of apprenticeship has a credential that recognizes both the foundational and specialized learning gained, and this enables the person to pursue whatever career options open up in the future.

In the United Kingdom, there is even an apprenticeship for people who design and implement apprenticeships. This apprenticeship, called Professional Development for Work-based Learning Practitioners, prepares individuals for careers in an industry that employs more than 30,000 people in the U.K. Apprentices become instructional designers, teachers and trainers, advisors and guidance counselors, and program evaluators. The apprenticeship is a great example of the combination of knowledge, skills, and abilities that human work requires. (Apprentices are expected to "demonstrate a 'can-do' attitude, numeracy, literacy and communication skills, and knowledge and experience in an occupational sector.")

Clearly, what we're seeing here is something beyond our traditional view of apprenticeships, but perhaps not in the way we might first assume. It's not the broad combination of learning that makes these new apprenticeships innovative—through the centuries, apprentices have always learned much more than a trade through the experience.

What's different about these apprenticeships is that the learning is transparent and recognized with a degree or other credential. This makes apprentices better able to respond and adapt to the inevitable changes in work that they will experience throughout their lives. By making their learning clear to all potential employers and education providers, it gives them the flexibility to use their learning as a foundation for whatever career pathways they want to pursue. It also makes it possible to "engineer" apprenticeship programs to meet a much wider range of needs and to take advantage of learning resources wherever they are—in the workplace, in academic institutions, or anywhere else people learn.

These new models of apprenticeships are spreading throughout the world. The European Commission, through its European Alliance for Apprenticeships, has established permeability between technical learning and other educational pathways as the standard for high-performing apprenticeships. Australia has several degree apprenticeships, including one leading to a diploma in information technology and financial services managed by PricewaterhouseCoopers, and another focused on high-level technical skills in engineering, technology, and innovation at the bachelor's degree level—with an option to continue to the master's—that was jointly developed by Siemens and Swinburne University of Technology.[10] Australia plans to greatly expand these programs, making them a model for work-based learning. Even Germany is moving in this direction with new dual programs leading to academic degrees with technical certifications.

While apprenticeships lag in the United States, the interest in creating more modern models is certainly there.[11] With funding from the U.S. Department of Labor, a number of community colleges have established apprenticeship programs with local employers, and California community colleges have established the California Apprenticeship Initiative with the ambitious goal of placing a million workers in jobs with an occupational associate degree in industries such as renewable energy, manufacturing, health care, and information and communication technologies.[12]

So why is the number of apprentices and apprenticeship opportunities in the United States lower than in many other countries? It's not as if people don't like or want apprenticeships—92% of Americans have a favorable view of them, 84% say more people should consider them, and 68% wish they themselves knew more about available opportunities for apprenticeships.[13] The answer may be that it's simply not a national priority in the United States compared with other nations. It's time for a concerted national effort to expand apprenticeships, particularly modern degree apprenticeships that combine the best of technical and academic learning and lead to a recognized credential that can be taken anywhere.

Apprenticeships are not the entire way to think about the merging of work and learning, but they offer important insights into how best to prepare people for a world of human work. In an apprenticeship, learning and being employed happen together—and that's the way it should work for all kinds of learning that people get throughout their lives. But for now, our education systems are divorced from work—or if *divorced* is too strong a word, let's just say education and work have grown apart and now have separate bedrooms.

The Merging of Work and Learning

Most colleges and universities rightly care about whether their students find work and are successful. Yet we still believe education and work are separate activities that happen in different settings. That may not have been a problem when work and education were so distinct—indeed, some undoubtedly saw it as an advantage. But in a world of human work, this forced separation creates a range of problems. Work offers excellent opportunities for the kind of active, engaged learning that develops higher-level thinking skills and human traits. It's also true that when virtually everyone needs to be learning continuously, a system in which learning and being employed are separate is unworkable.

But all this is changing, and in the new human work ecosystem, people are not defined as "students" or "employees" moving back and forth between discrete systems. Instead, people are "worker-learners" because learning and working happen together and are, in fact, inseparable. In the human work ecosystem, we need to think beyond the traditional actors and categories that we know. Learning and work are now intertwined in ways that few in these systems seem to understand or appreciate.

Jim Wolford, the chief executive officer of the information technology company Atomic Data in Minneapolis, saw that focusing on the individual both as learner and worker was key. Wolford had a business problem—difficulty in finding talented employees to fill vacancies at his company. But unlike many business leaders, he saw that his business problem was at its core a social problem—the lack of economic opportunity for people of color in Minnesota. So, he decided to address both problems.

Atomic Data had made a commitment to diversify its workforce six years ago, and now roughly one-third of its 200 employees are people of color. But Wolford wasn't satisfied with

this result. He realized that simply relying on the flow of graduates from universities, community colleges, and trade schools
in his region was not providing him with either the number
or the quality of people he needed for his business. "It wasn't
working for us or our customers, so we decided to do it ourselves," Wolford said. Atomic decided to partner with a local
community-based vocational training and job placement program called Summit Academy OIC, whose mission statement
could be the title of a book: "The best social service program in
the world is a job."

Within nine months, Wolford and Summit CEO Louis King
had designed an intensive, twenty-week program for IT technicians, and five months later, in late 2018, the first class graduated. Screening for the program is extensive. Of the 142 people
who applied for the first class, 115 were rejected, either because
they had failed one or both screening tests (in general knowledge
and computer literacy) or they had criminal histories that dis-
qualify potential workers in the security-conscious IT field. The
program stresses general business tenets as well as specific skills
that would be needed in their jobs, Wolford said. "We wanted to
train them so they would be ready to go on the first day of the
job," he observed.

In the first class, eight dropped out, often because of challenges such as finding child care or transportation, Wolford said.
But of the eighteen who graduated, sixteen were immediately
hired by Atomic for full-time positions paying slightly less than
$40,000 a year, with benefits.

Linus Onuoha has one of those jobs, as an operations center
technician monitoring the devices of Atomic's clients for potential problems. A native of Nigeria, Onuoha moved with his family to the Twin Cities when he was 7. He graduated from high
school, earned a bachelor's degree while on a soccer scholarship
in college, and then joined the National Guard. But after finish-
ing his Guard training, he couldn't find a job he liked. He worked
as a security guard in apartment buildings before learning about

the new Atomic-Summit training program. Now, he has a steady job with an opportunity for advancement.

"I'm definitely a lot better off than where I was earlier," said Onuoha, who is in his late 20s. "I have a map of where I want to be in a few years, and this gives me a clear vision of how to get there." De'Angelo Parker agreed. A fellow graduate of the first training class at Atomic, Parker had taught himself enough about electronics to open his own business. He had clients, but he learned that owning a small business could be challenging and his income erratic. "My business was running fine, but I never pass on an opportunity to learn more," said Parker, who is in his mid-30s.

He said he was drawn to the Atomic-Summit program because it was free. The company and the academy split the cost, Wolford said, with investments by Atomic and grants and donations directed to the program through Summit. Hired by Atomic out of the first training class, Parker now works as a service technician, with a steady, predictable salary and benefits that help him and his family, including seven children. Primarily self-taught for years after graduating from high school, Parker said the certificate he received from the Atomic program "is another notch in my belt" that will help him advance his career.

Wolford said his experience with the first class taught him that he probably will have to offer other support services to address issues such as homelessness, inadequate transportation, and a lack of child care options—all things that can derail trainees. And he will likely have to interest other businesses in hiring the program's graduates, because Atomic, while growing by 30% a year, will not be able to continue to hire such a high percentage of graduates.

The program "has been wildly successful," Wolford said. "The graduates are doing well. They are all people with high IQs, but they never would have had this opportunity because of the color of their skin or their locale." Some of the first group of graduates have already been promoted, he said. Within two to three years, some could be making $100,000 annually, with no college degree required. In a labor market where it's tough to find people with the right skills, "we need these workers as much as they need us," Wolford said. "It's great to do something good. But I'm a capitalist and entrepreneur. I'm trying to solve the needs of my clients. It's great to help my clients and help people," he said with a laugh. "But I'm trying to make money, and also get into Valhalla."

Atomic Data understands the deeper connection between learning and work, and how investing in the talent of people is the key to success in a world of human work. A few very large companies—including Amazon, Starbucks, and Verizon—have also come to understand that developing the broad talent of their people helps the company in innumerable ways and is reflected in the bottom line.

The Lee Company of Nashville, Tennessee, also understands how earning and learning are merging. The company has a simple mission statement: "To create a workplace where our employees can thrive." Founded in 1944, the family-owned heating, air-conditioning, plumbing, and electrical business has thrived over the years, growing into a company with approximately $225 million in annual revenue and about 1,500 employees. But as the construction trade business began to wane at the beginning of the Great Recession of the late 2000s, the company decided it had to step up its efforts to improve the skills of its workers to remain competitive in an increasingly difficult market.

So, like a lot of companies, it created its own training program to bolster the knowledge and skills of its workers. Previously, the company had depended on trade association training programs before deciding these programs were not doing the job. Unlike other companies, however, its training system is a free, structured four-year program that leads to an industry-recognized certification and journeyman license. As the firm's recruiting materials say, the credential "is yours for life. Take it wherever you want. Of course, we'd love for you to stay at Lee Company, but even if you don't, we want to set you up for success." In fact, company officials call their program the Lee Company University to reflect its focus on developing the talent of their workers.

"Skilled labor; that's our product," said Richard Perko, one of the architects of the program. He was named president and chief executive officer of the company after the previous CEO, Bill Lee, was elected governor of Tennessee in 2018. "We needed a better way to train our workers." During the training program's first twelve years, 1,258 classes were completed by Lee workers, many of whom took multiple courses. In addition to courses leading to certification in one of the trades needed by Lee, the training program partners with seven colleges and universities to offer opportunities to learn leadership, computers, and other fields.

Jody Wood is one of those students who sees the value the courses offer to him and to the company. Since joining Lee in 2011, he's completed four separate training courses, in HVAC, welding, project management, and electrical. He's also taught courses in plumbing, pipe-fitting, and welding. That has meant spending as many as four nights a week at Lee Company University, but Wood believes it's been well worth the effort.

"It's made me more versatile, and I've grown in value to the company," said Wood, who is in his early 50s and now a plumbing foreman on Lee's large construction projects. "The more you know, the farther you go." He encourages all young employees he works with to sign up for the classes, telling younger workers that adding skills can help them protect their futures.

Wood should know. A former truck driver and U.S. Air Force veteran, he worked for a variety of construction trade businesses, two of which (a plumbing company and a swimming pool installer) went out of business during the recession. "I'm happy I found Lee Company," Wood said. "I've been in a few other companies, and this is one of the best. They treat you like family."

The training program helps employees to keep up with new materials and methods used in the industry and to enhance skills that can lead to productive careers. "Part of our mission is to bring out the best they can be," Perko, the CEO, said. "Maybe they're not going to be president of the company, but they might be the best welder they can be. I can find an engineer at any time, but finding a good welder can be really tough."

Perko said most graduates of the company's training program choose to stay with Lee. But the ones who decide to leave can still offer greater contributions to the whole construction-trade industry, he said. "People ask me sometimes, 'What happens if you train them and they leave?'" he said. "But we say, 'What if you don't train them and they stay?'"

An even deeper integration of learning and work is on the horizon. Consider the case of Catalyte, a software development company that has developed an entirely new approach to identifying and developing talent and built their business model around it. At first glance, Catalyte looks like a software development company—it takes on projects from Fortune 1000 companies such as Nike, AT&T, Blue Cross Blue Shield, and many others, and assigns them to teams of software programmers. While all companies in the software development industry have traditionally dealt with shortages of programmers with the skills and abilities needed in a dynamic, fast-paced, and highly technical environment, Catalyte's founder, Michael Rosenbaum, saw something that others had not. His insight was that addressing the shortages of programmers was not a business challenge to be overcome but a business opportunity to be exploited.[14]

Rosenbaum believed that many people from underrepresented populations were being excluded from consideration as programmers. He saw that they were not lacking in innate ability—it was just that both education systems and employers were more focused on cultural markers than what really mattered. He sensed that if Catalyte could identify people who had been overlooked and help them learn what they needed to be successful, it would give his company a tremendous competitive advantage.

So Catalyte developed an assessment of the attributes associated with successful programmers and made it available to anyone to take for free. The hundreds of thousands of applicants who have taken the assessment provide Catalyte with a wealth of data to refine the model and extend his company's hiring edge. Candidates identified by the assessment are placed into a five-month onboarding program that leads to jobs with the company paying $40,000 to start and usually increasing to $75,000 or more after two years.

The company hires all kinds of people who are overlooked by many employers. They range from ages 17 to 72 and include immigrants, truck drivers, health care workers, and people from the skilled trades. Many of the people the company hires are unemployed and, by prevailing standards, unemployable in any job that could pay a decent wage. Catalyte teaches new hires both technical coding skills and "soft" skills to deal with clients. The firm also helps them go to college to gain associate and other degrees.

Catalyte's CEO, Jacob Hsu, described the company's objective this way: "We want to kill pedigree. We're proving it now with software developers. Our goal is to do this across industries so that we can make a much more diverse, egalitarian workforce, where everybody gets a shot if they can prove that they have the potential." Let's not be coy about this—Catalyte's process eliminates bias against candidates in the selection process who for racial or cultural reasons have less familiarity with navigating the hiring process, and it allows the company to tap into a pool of talent other firms don't believe exists.[15]

Catalyte's approach is scalable—it has already hired more than 1,700 people and is operating in five cities around the United States. Many of the graduates of the program go on to jobs and careers in other companies. While Catalyte began with the idea that a new approach could open opportunities to people who were shut out of the current system, the firm has also found this approach works better for clients, who report that Catalyte's teams outperform software developers from other companies that rely on the usual models.

Catalyte shows the power of shifting employers to true learning and talent-based business models. ?

But it's not just these new approaches to skills development for cutting-edge technology that show the way forward to the future of human work. Some of the best models go back centuries, but they can still serve as models for how to meet today's and tomorrow's needs. Take for example the City and Guilds of London Institute, an institution founded 140 years ago by sixteen livery companies (guilds) and the City of London.

Today, students there learn ancient crafts such as stone carving, gilding, and woodcarving, with much of the learning taking place under master craftspeople in cathedrals and other historical structures throughout the region. But they also learn constantly evolving technical skills, such as laser scanning and imaging, along with communication skills (for teaching and explaining work to the public) and organizational and management skills. They also develop the most human trait of all—their creativity. The devastating 2019 fire at Cathedrale Notre-Dame de Paris brought into focus how relevant and necessary these artisans are to our society, and how the work is deeply rewarding to those who perform it.

The Learning Organization

When work is learning and learning is work, employers and educators are in the same business. Employers need to embrace their role as developers of talent and not expect this to be someone else's problem or responsibility. This shift really requires a change in attitudes, as well as a whole new set of organizational capacities to support learning. As always, it's a question of scale—many employers support learning, but few really understand what it means to be a learning organization.

When Trish Holliday was promoted to be chief learning officer with the state of Tennessee in 2012, her title was new in Tennessee and unique in the nation. She had joined Tennessee's government as a training officer in 2005 after working for years in a ministry with her father in Appalachia. She immediately embraced the challenge of helping an enterprise with such a broad and diverse mission to attract and retain talented employees. "That's when I began to realize that my life's work was to help people reach full potential," she said.

State government is the largest public employer in Tennessee, with approximately 42,000 workers in ninety-five counties and twenty-three different cabinet agencies. In her early days in government, Holliday said, training for employees was an event, one day here or there on the calendar, usually scheduled for compliance purposes. But Holliday had other ideas. "My dream was to make the entire state of Tennessee a learning organization," she said. That meant creating a more centralized learning environment to leverage training resources and create a more collaborative atmosphere, bringing together workers from different departments to learn together and share best practices.

That work received a new boost after Bill Haslam was elected governor in 2010. He established a goal of making Tennessee the best state in the Southeast for quality jobs and named a chief learning officer, the first such statewide job in the nation.

Tennessee state government has created twenty-eight different state leadership academies, ranging from management training for established employees to programs to groom younger employees for future leadership positions. The results have been impressive, Holliday said. Turnover rates have declined. Veteran workers who might have left government have stayed. Younger workers who viewed government as a first job and a launching pad to another career stuck around. But most important, Holliday said, Tennessee government has experienced "a cultural change so that training is not seen as event driven but as a continuous process. We want to recognize workplace learning to be a daily thing, not an event on the calendar."

The merging of work and learning is about more than education and training—it also has the potential to transform organizations in fundamental ways. John Hagel III and John Seely Brown write about organizations needing to make the shift away from a <u>focus on scaling</u> *efficiency* to <u>one on scaling</u> *learning*: "We're not talking about sharing existing knowledge more effectively (although there's certainly a lot of opportunity there). In a world of exponential change, <u>existing knowledge depreciates at an accelerating rate</u>. The most powerful learning in this kind of world involves creating new knowledge. This kind of learning does not occur in a training room; it occurs on the job, in the day-to-day work environment." They go on to suggest that learning organizations harness <u>digital technologies to augment the capabilities of people rather than replace them.</u>[16]

Lumina Foundation commissioned the global consulting company Accenture to conduct an analysis of the return on investment of one type of program—tuition assistance—that organizations can use to become true learning organizations. While not uncommon, tuition assistance is seen by most companies as a benefit for employees and therefore counts as part of the overall compensation expense. Accenture found that the cost of education for employees at several different companies studied was more than offset by direct financial returns from higher rates of retention, increased productivity, and other benefits to the companies studied.[17] Stated simply, the bottom line literally improved because the companies invested in talent.

We need to consider how to help employers make this significant shift to becoming learning organizations. It would help if we realize that this <u>shift changes the business model of most companies</u>, and that it requires a very significant—and permanent—investment of resources. It would help if we understood that investment in talent is no different from investment in physical facilities, machinery, or any other asset. Like these physical assets, <u>investing in people is justified by its ROI</u>. It needs to be made consistently over time, just as the return on investment also happens over years.

But this is not how most investments in talent development are treated by either employers or government. They're usually seen as an expense, albeit a deductible one—and thus one that still hurts the bottom line rather than helps it. We need to rethink everything from tax policy to accounting standards to make sure investing in people is seen as essential to the enterprise, and not as a well-intentioned—but ultimately expendable—benefit to employees.

Learning Organizations, Communities, and the Virtuous Cycle

Lumina Foundation's analysis of the ROI of tuition assistance found an additional outcome of these programs that deserves recognition—they help build stronger communities.[18] In this book, I have referred to human work as a virtuous cycle of earning, learning, and serving. I believe that the presence of that virtuous cycle is indicative of true learning organizations. I also believe that the best way to see it in action is in the effect learning organizations have on the communities where they are located.

In Chapter 1, I talked about Joel Lewis, who works alongside collaborative robots—cobots—in a Cummins plant in southern Indiana. Cummins is a good example of an industrial enterprise that has achieved marketplace success by embracing human work and its role as a learning organization. A manufacturer of diesel engines and modern power-generation products, Cummins has grown from modest Midwestern roots to become a global company, with more than $26 billion in annual sales and 60,000 employees in the United States, China, India, the United Kingdom, and other countries.

But it still invests in small towns in Indiana, including Seymour, a city of about 20,000 just south of Columbus, where Cummins was founded in 1919.

In the mid-1970s, Cummins purchased a plot of land near the CSX railroad tracks on the east side of Seymour that used to be the city dump. For decades, it had been home to Arvin Industries, a manufacturer of exhaust pipes and mufflers for American automakers such as Ford, General Motors, and Studebaker. Old photos in the county archives show scenes of workers in a dimly lit factory operating huge metal stamping and molding machines.

But now, that same land is home to Cummins's Seymour Technical Center and Seymour Engine Plant, which together employ more than 1,000 workers to design and build some of the largest and most technologically advanced diesel engines in the world, with 80% of them sold to customers outside the United States. Seymour's main product is the QSK95 engine, nicknamed the Hedgehog. The engine is 8 feet high and 14 feet long, with sixteen cylinders, capable of generating 4,000 horsepower. Sold at prices up to $1 million each, it is used in locomotives, boats, and mining trucks, and on offshore oil and gas platforms. A quaint town, which has promoted itself for years as The Crossroads of Southern Indiana, Seymour is now the center of an international business.

"We are very focused on innovation and how to use technology to improve our products," said Elizabeth Hoegeman, Cummins's executive director of global manufacturing engineering. That work involves using cobots and other new technologies, but also additive manufacturing, which uses lasers and 3-D printers to model new parts or create replacement parts, and machine learning and advanced analytics to discover more efficient manufacturing processes. Technology has opened new opportunities for the company's human workforce.

The longtime executive director of the Jackson County Industrial Development Corporation, Jim Plump, said the company's decision "to locate Project Hedgehog in Seymour can't really be measured in jobs and investment only." While investing $300 million in Seymour facilities in the last decade, the company has also worked "to create partnerships to improve education, amenities, and overall quality of life so Cummins and other industries would be able to attract the level of talent needed." Those partnerships have led to improved pre-kindergarten offerings in Seymour, more walking and bicycling trails, and a renewed emphasis on the Seymour Main Street program to draw more businesses downtown, Plump said.[19]

Cummins is well known for its investments in improving learning opportunities in the communities in which it operates, and not just for its workers.[20] But what I find most interesting is that Cummins involves its workers directly in these efforts as teachers and mentors, as well as integrating them with the company's day-to-day operations through internships, apprenticeships, and job-shadowing opportunities. Workers can do service projects on company time, and in 2016, more than 70% of Cummins's workers actively participated in projects in its communities.[21]

Cummins's efforts deserve emulation. Indeed, many other companies have similar programs and numerous people throughout the world serve their communities, whether or not their employers support and encourage it. But I do believe Cummins's experience shows how the three elements of human work—earning, learning, and serving—come together and how organizations need to organize themselves to support all three.

Changing Our View of Work

The emergence of human work with its elements of earning, learning, and serving has cultural implications for educators, too. Most still see work and learning as separate activities—and believe they should remain so.[22] Worse, there are those who believe that a focus on work somehow demeans learning because it is practical or "enriches" the person who does it. This prejudice is deeply rooted, and we also see it in the distinction between applied science and basic science (many call it "pure" science) that is taken for granted and can be seen reflected in the status accorded faculty members on almost any university campus. I don't know the source of this academic prejudice against work, but it needs to go away.

As we've seen, the nature of human work makes clear that learning is an integral component of work, as is service. Even thinking of learning as preparation for work is obsolete—today it is just as true that not only does work lead to learning, but much of the value of work lies in the learning that grows out of it. It is time to bring these worlds together in a human work ecosystem in which everyone has the opportunity for meaningful work—earning, learning, and serving—throughout life.

But how else would a change this major and meaningful affect our society? It's not hard to imagine that creating a people-centered economy based on human work and assuring that everyone can be prepared for it would have profound effects on our society beyond jobs and the economy. It is not just work and jobs that have been affected by technology. Civic life throughout the world also has changed dramatically in recent years. AI holds the promise, or more ominously the threat, to transform civil society, and perhaps even democracy itself, in ways we can scarcely imagine. I believe building the systems that support human work may offer us a way forward.

Human Work in a Democratic Society

"Curious, how often you humans manage to obtain that
which you do not want."
— Mr. Spock, *Star Trek*, "Errand of Mercy"

By late 2011, after more than thirty years in government and
public affairs, Erich Mische decided he wanted to do something
new. "I had had enough of D.C. and enough of politics and government," he said. "I needed something different."

A Minnesota native, Mische had served as a city council member in White Bear Lake, spent more than a decade working for
the state legislature and worked as a top aide to Norm Coleman
during Coleman's tenures as mayor of St. Paul and as a U.S. sena-
tor. After four years in Coleman's Senate office, Mische joined a
bipartisan public affairs firm in Washington, D.C., while playing a key role in Coleman's re-election campaign. When Coleman lost his Senate seat, Mische joined another lobbying firm in
Washington.

Mische had a good job, but he felt something was missing.
Once he decided to make a change, he wasn't sure what he
wanted to do. But he soon learned that the Minnesota nonprofit
Spare Key, whose board he served on, was looking for a new
executive director. He had been involved with the organization
since a communications class he was teaching at the University

of St. Thomas had decided to help Spare Key with a branding campaign. "I'll be perfectly candid. This was not on my radar screen," he said. But he took the job when it was offered, moved his family back to Minnesota, and got to work at Spare Key, whose mission is to help families with a critically ill or seriously injured family member.

Now based in Minneapolis, the nonprofit was founded in 1997 by Patsy and Robb Keech when their son Derian struggled through six major surgeries and five open-heart surgeries in two years because of a genetic birth defect. Family, friends, and even strangers helped the family pay its mortgage during those years. After Derian died, Patsy and Robb decided to start a charity to help families in similar situations.

The high purpose was inspiring, but Mische soon learned the actual work of a nonprofit was hard. Very hard. "After six months, I decided it was the worst decision I'd ever made," he said. "It was sobering and humbling" because he thought all the contacts and skills he had developed in public service would "magically transfer into the nonprofit world." But as soon as he realized "it was going to take a lot of hard work," he worked even harder. As a former Senate chief of staff, he was accustomed to having staff members do his schedule, arrange his travel, and perform other tasks for him. But in a small nonprofit, "you are the chief cook and bottle washer. You do everything." If there was a direct mail fund-raising piece, he would review the copy and then put the mailing labels on it. Fund-raising, advocacy, communications—he did it all.

After inheriting a $300,000 annual budget, he helped grow the organization to a $1.2 million operation. "All of the skills I had acquired in past roles were very important and translated into this job," he said. "Without a doubt, everything I learned to that point goes into everything I do every day."

But he wanted to do more. That's when, three years ago, a friend invited him to attend a retreat with the British entrepreneur Richard Branson. The topic: the exponential power of technology to change lives. After that session, Mische realized that, to serve more families, Spare Key's business model needed to change. "For the past twenty years, our business model was the same as every nonprofit" using standard approaches for fund-raising. "Under that model, we could only help hundreds of families with hundreds of thousands or a low million dollars," he said.

With the support of his board, Mische helped develop a new model to "harness technology so we can grow our resources exponentially so we can serve more families." Spare Key established a proprietary online crowdfunding platform, where potential donors are offered the choice of either donating directly to a family in need or donating to Spare Key. If a donor chooses to directly support a family, 100% of the donation goes to that purpose. That allows families to receive assistance beyond help with mortgages (Spare Key's traditional method of assistance) and helps families pay for other expenses, such as car payments and utility bills.

"I now believe we're on the verge of helping unlimited numbers of families," he said. "Under the old business model, we could only scratch the surface."

Spare Key is working to build out a marketing and awareness campaign to drive more donors to its site. The organization may also license the use of the platform technology to other nonprofits, producing fees to support Spare Key's work. Originally serving only residents of Minnesota, Spare Key now helps families in Wisconsin and North and South Dakota. In the near future, Mische expects "to be operating in pretty much every state in the union." When that happens, Spare Key "will essentially become a software company dedicated to philanthropy." A lot of work remains, but Mische is confident that "three years from now, the budget can be in the tens of millions and the families we serve will be in the tens of thousands."

And that will be a great public service, a goal Mische has long pursued. "I got into government and politics as a young man because I wanted to change the world," said Mische, now in his mid-50s. "I wanted to do public service, and what I do today is an extension of public service. I believe we all have an obligation to our fellow citizens to see that they are better off."

When I heard Mische's story, I knew it embodied much of what I was trying to articulate about human work. Is Mische's work how he earns the money he needs to live and support his family? Is it a learning experience through which he develops his personal abilities, new skills, and knowledge about the world around him? Is it an opportunity to be of service to others—something that has always been important in his life? Of course, the answers to these questions are yes, yes, and yes.

Human work draws on everything that makes us human. It's not simply what people bring to work that is important—it's also the meaning of work that matters. Does it matter? Does it make a difference in people's lives? These are the questions that Mische asked about his work that took him in a different direction. I find it interesting—and important—that meaningful work is often work that requires us to use more of our abilities and drives us to keep learning.

Work and the Social Fabric

We have already seen how the loss of meaningful work affects people in ways far beyond the purely economic. Just as human work brings meaning to our lives, when people lose the opportunity to work, they can turn fearful and even angry. They can feel left behind and left out—disconnected from their communities and the broader life of the nation.

These effects are measurable and well documented. A meta-analysis of research on the effects of long-term unemployment showed that rates of suffering from a range of psychological problems are more than double for unemployed versus employed individuals—34% to 16%.[1] Working-class men are particularly vulnerable to the psychological effects of job loss, but all suffer from higher rates of depression, anxiety, and lower self-esteem. Furthermore, a causal link between unemployment and social alienation has been established through research.[2]

But it's not just the unemployed who are at risk. The anthropologist David Graeber wrote a best-seller on what he calls "bullshit jobs"—jobs that even the people who hold them believe have no value whatsoever.[3] The situation he describes sounds almost comic, except that it's based on solid research that up to 40% of workers feel their jobs make no meaningful contribution to society. Many felt their jobs could be eliminated and no one would know the difference. We need to better understand how we got into this situation and what it means for our future as a society. It can't be good.

I have argued that, like other technological innovations that preceded it, artificial intelligence will not lead to the end of work and indeed will create many new opportunities for human work for those with the requisite skills and abilities. But the effect of AI on the workforce is not completely benign. This is a dynamic area for research, but recent findings support a more nuanced view of the effects of automation and AI on jobs—positive for some, but negative for others. As technology transforms occupations, requiring higher levels of knowledge, skills, and abilities, many workers are being pushed into lower-productivity sectors of the economy, such as health care and building services, in which wages are low and the pressure to keep them low is fierce.[4]

This helps explain the paradox of how technology-driven increases in productivity across the economy are now accompanied by wage stagnation for many workers and a growing divide between workers who are moving forward in wages and opportunities for work and those who are left behind.[5] In our society, where work is so closely associated with feelings of worth and value, the implications of this growing divide are profound and frightening.

Technology and Social Division

To understand the broader ways technology is changing our society, we should start with the elephant in the room—politics. This book is apolitical in the sense that the issues it addresses and the solutions it posits transcend partisan politics. But there is no denying that the divide between those who can take advantage of the new opportunities created by technological change and those who are marginalized by it, whether employed or not, already has had a disruptive effect on politics throughout the world.

These effects have even been quantified through research. In regions where there are high levels of occupational vulnerability and associated worker anxiety about the future, voters are more likely to support candidates who promise radical change.[6] In the United States, one region where these effects are dramatic is the Upper Midwest. This region used to have a strong economy based on well-paid manufacturing jobs, coupled with low levels of educational achievement. When those jobs went away after 2008, and the people who held them couldn't find anything equivalent, the effects were devastating—both individually and socially. These effects are reflected in the politics of the region, and several states in the Midwest that were known for their stable politics are now crucial swing states in national elections.

At the same time, other regions are experiencing very different consequences from the changing economy and evolving work environment. Some regions are thriving—their economies are strong, populations are growing, and job prospects are plentiful, at least for those with the necessary qualifications. Some of these places find themselves in a positive cycle where strong economies allow them to make investments that improve the quality of life of the community, which in turn makes them even more attractive to employers seeking talent.

Experts such as Bruce Katz and Richard Florida have chronicled these trends and suggest that while the red state–blue state divide in the United States has been overstated, an overriding factor about these thriving regions is the people who live there are better educated. This is reflected not just in a very different job market, but also in different social and political attitudes.[7]

It's hard to believe the divisions in our society could be any worse than they already are, which is why we should be worried by the research suggesting that the red-blue political divide among U.S. states and cities centered on levels of economic prosperity may indeed become even more pronounced.[8] Technology's ongoing effect on jobs will do much to explain why. At least some of these effects on politics can only be described as toxic, including creating a fertile ground for those who believe that their problems were caused by immigrants, better-educated "elites," or women, or result from conspiracies that people are out to get them.

Of course, not everyone who has suffered from the massive economic shifts over the past ten years has fallen prey to extremism, but it's undeniable that views that were considered extreme only a few years ago have moved into the political mainstream. The result is that our society, as reflected by our politics, is far more polarized than before the Great Recession.

But what's happening to jobs is not the full story of how technology is changing politics and our democracy. Changes in work ripple through society, just as the rapid disruption of print and television journalism go far beyond the loss of jobs in local newspapers and TV stations. But AI is also transforming society more broadly as its power to direct the flow of information, shape public opinion, network like-minded individuals, and reinforce belief is developed and exploited. The way people obtain and process information about the world around them has completely changed, and this affects not just our politics, but also the full range of interactions and relationships that define society—from the most personal to the most global. Indeed, AI and technology are just as transformative of civil society as they are of the economy, perhaps even more so.

As in the case of work, AI's effect on civil society can be positive, particularly by creating new kinds of social networks, democratizing access to data and information, and mobilizing collective action. But AI can also have malignant effects by enabling people to remain in self-imposed isolation—not just physically, but intellectually and emotionally as well.

Just a few years ago, the realization that technology would make information widely and almost instantaneously available was seen as leveling the playing field and spreading democracy and civic participation. Not only would access to information be made universal, it was hoped that technology would open the doors to new participation in civic life by giving voice to those who had been excluded and allowing people to tell their own stories in their own voices.

Few anticipated that technology would, in many ways, have the opposite effect. Rather than opening people to new viewpoints and perspectives, technology has made it possible for people to live within bubbles where the only information they receive supports their existing worldview and prejudices. Artificial intelligence allows—indeed encourages—information flows to become more one-sided as people naturally gravitate to sources that are aligned with their existing views. It's telling that this shift coincides with the collapse of local journalism, and with it, the informed decision making and public accountability a watchdog press provides. The solutions to this problem are beyond the scope of this book,[9] but it is essential to assure that more people can distinguish fact from fiction and make informed and critical decisions about the public issues that affect them.

There are even more worrisome consequences of people having their perspective of the world shaped by algorithms. AI has contributed to creating an environment in which "fake news" can flourish. Politics is not the only arena that is suffering the consequences. As a direct result of the ease at which falsehoods can be spread, and the willingness of many to believe them, we are now seeing the resurgence of measles, which was close to eradication just a few years ago.[10]

And it gets worse. The combination of big data and social media allows those who wish to influence the political process to do so with remarkable efficiency—whether for benevolent or malevolent ends. What makes technology so powerful in politics is that it can be used to influence the views and beliefs of millions of people at a time. But it is more effective at inflaming passions than promoting rational and deliberate consideration of diverse viewpoints to reach a political consensus.

It's hard to believe we could be nostalgic for a time when lobbyists and power brokers in smoke-filled rooms exerted undue influence over political decisions. But today, it seems impossible to know whether our core political views—and those of our fellow citizens—are being manipulated, or by whom.

We are living in dangerous times. Our politics have become defined by rigid and incompatible positions on virtually every important issue. While we've long believed, as an episode of *Star Wars: The Clone Wars*, once put it, that "compromise is a virtue to be cultivated, not a weakness to be despised," the fact is that compromise is becoming more difficult as positions on issues take on the wrappings of morality. Researchers have found that the U.S. Congress is more polarized today that at any time since the Civil War.[11] Sadly, the only time many are truly confronted by beliefs different from their own is through social media interactions with family or friends. Indeed, the data suggest that many people would rather end a relationship than believe they can get along with people who disagree with them. One in six Americans has stopped talking to a family member or close friend because of the 2016 presidential election.[12]

There is abundant evidence that technology—specifically AI and big data—is contributing to this problem and making it worse. While there has never been more information available to people, the way people manage this flood is ironically limiting rather than expanding the range of perspectives that they are exposed to. Search engine and social media platform algorithms now determine the news we receive, the analyses of issues and viewpoints we see, and the data and evidence we're presented.[13] It's not an exaggeration to say that people can now live in separate realities based on their pre-existing beliefs.

Arthur Brooks, a *Washington Post* columnist and former president of the American Enterprise Institute, has written on this issue with insight and passion. He argues that technology can be exploited by media, advocates, politicians, despots, and anyone else seeking power and influence. They use the power of technology to inflame passions by feeding people a one-sided argument that they are "good" and "right" and those on the other side are "bad" and "wrong." Through this process those with different views become not just the opposition, but the enemy. What Brooks calls the "outrage industrial complex" doesn't just pollute our civic life, it creates a form of addiction that, like all addictions, is extremely difficult to escape.

Until now, it's fair to say that AI and technology have tended to make people more passive participants in society. Too many have lost the ability to play an active role in the economy as AI has disrupted the workplace. Too many have become passive consumers of information and are living in self-imposed bubbles of belief. And too many have withdrawn into passive lives of isolation apart from any meaningful engagement in their communities or, in some cases, even their families.

How does one escape the temptations of an AI-created bubble of information and belief? The answer, obviously, is to burst the bubble—to escape by being exposed to ideas and experiences that are fundamentally different from our own.

This begins by being exposed to people who are different from us—who have different beliefs, values, cultures, and life experiences. Human work offers this chance because it is built on human attributes such as empathy, openness, and flexibility—precisely those needed for strong communities and a strong society. The results we need to assure through human work are not just higher incomes but also openness to different cultures, willingness to engage individuals with different ideologies and perspectives, increased likelihood to vote and volunteer, and recognition of the value of open markets and free, democratic systems of government. The characteristics of human work have much more than economic consequences; they are the lifeblood of free people and societies.

Overcoming Authoritarianism

When considering human work and the future of democracy, it's impossible to avoid the rise of authoritarianism throughout the world. According to new research from the Georgetown University Center on Education and the Workforce, the alarming increase of authoritarianism on a global scale can't be considered in isolation.[14]

The postwar world order was based on the expectation in the West that democracy was spreading throughout the world, country by country, and would eventually become the preferred form of government everywhere. Foreign relations were based on the broad consensus that established democracies should be vigilant and unwavering in offering military and cultural support to emerging democracies. Democracy spread throughout Latin America and even appeared likely to take root in China. The end of the Cold War seemed to confirm the inevitability of democracy's spread, with only a few old-style authoritarian systems left in Cuba, North Korea, and other poor, isolated countries.

Today, the tide seems to be turning in the opposite direction. Authoritarianism—particularly in the form of populist nationalism—has returned to Russia and parts of Eastern Europe, Asia, and Latin America. China appears resolute in maintaining state control over political and cultural expression. And we now understand clearly that not even the United States and Western Europe are immune from authoritarianism's allure.

Of course, much of that allure is based on fear—fear of change, fear of loss of advantage, fear of the other. Authoritarian leaders and wannabes exploit this fear by appealing to group identity and cohesion and by defining those who appear different as a threat. We should recognize that authoritarianism is not just imposed from above—at least, not at first. It is an individual worldview that everyone to a greater or lesser extent is susceptible to. Research on authoritarianism supports the idea that preferences for conformity and social cohesion are among the psychological tendencies that predispose people toward preferring strong hierarchical leadership styles. In other words, individuals who have a greater preference for group cohesion are more inclined to feel threatened by diversity, be intolerant of outsiders, and react by supporting authoritarian leaders.[15]

With its preference for conformity, authoritarianism is a clear threat to liberal democracy and the diversity of expression, belief, and ways of living that it is designed to protect. But the same education system that prepares people for work can play a role in protecting our democratic way of life. Numerous studies going back decades and conducted throughout the world have shown that higher levels of education are inversely correlated with authoritarianism.[16]

Authoritarian attitudes are tracked by three major surveys—the World Values Survey, General Social Survey, and American National Election Studies. Data from all three show that higher levels of education reduce authoritarian attitudes and values.[17] Today, nearly a third of Americans who haven't gone to college believe that having a "strong leader" is good for the country, compared to only about 13% of those with a bachelor's degree.[18] Meanwhile, according to a 2017 Pew Research Center study, about a quarter of people with a high school diploma or less say "military rule would be a good way to govern our country." Only 7% of college grads support that view.[19]

Why does education thwart authoritarian attitudes? At its best, higher education strives to promote independent thought and critical examination of established orthodoxy, not to mention inquisitiveness and curiosity. All this stands in stark contrast to the blind acceptance of information and opinion from authorities. Higher education also exposes people to diverse ideas and cultures, showing that differences are not as bad or as dangerous as people may have been conditioned to believe. Education helps people to better understand abstract principles of democracy and equality and how to deal with complexity and differences in society.[20] Education also helps improve interpersonal communication skills—essential for civic participation in a democracy.

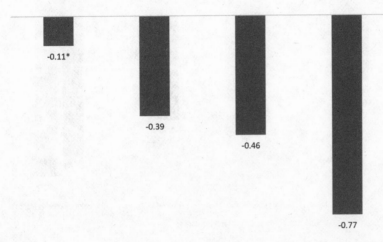

Figure 3. The more education people have, the less likely they are to hold authoritarian political attitudes.
Source: Georgetown University Center on Education and the Workforce regression analysis of data from the World Values Survey, 1994–2014.

But perhaps the most powerful reason education is an antidote to authoritarianism lies even deeper. People with higher levels of education are much less likely to be authoritarian in their child-rearing preferences than others.[21] The shift toward raising children who themselves are more tolerant, independent, and inquisitive may be education's most profound effect on society.

Of course, formal learning cannot on its own change the equation, but absent well-informed citizens who can critically judge the ideas and perspectives of those who hold office, the consequences will be chilling. When the president of the United States invents "facts" or tells outright lies, dismisses scientific evidence, and demonstrates a stunning ignorance of history, the consequences are real for those who have not developed their own critical-thinking capacities.

So, the greatest contribution of a better-educated population to shared prosperity is that educated citizens are the best defense against the threats to our democratic way of life. The debate about President Donald Trump's and others' perceived threats to democracy will linger, but for democracy to prosper in the long term, we need more people to reach higher levels of education.

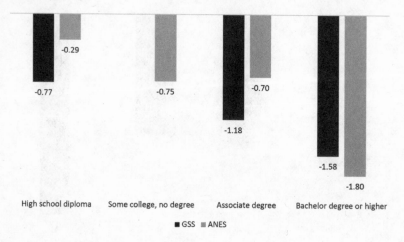

Figure 4. The more education people have, the less they prefer authoritarian qualities in children.
Source: Georgetown University Center on Education and the Workforce regression analysis of data from the General Social Survey, 1986–2016, and the American National Election Studies, 2000–2016.

U.S. college graduates display a remarkable consistency in their support for civic processes. More than four of every five people with master's degrees or higher and 68% of those with any college education voted in the 2016 election compared to about half of high school graduates and one-third of dropouts. This hasn't changed much going back to the 1980s, according to the United States Elections Project.[22] And voting is only one of the indicators. Almost 40% of Americans with a bachelor's degree or higher volunteer, compared to 16% of high school graduates and only 8% of high school dropouts.[23] They also contribute more to charity and are more likely to participate in community organizations such as schools and service and religious organizations. This is practically a truism—the positive effects of increased education on a panoply of social indicators has been repeatedly established by research all over the world.[24]

Volunteerism and charitable giving are not the only activities or trends affected by education. Higher levels of education are also associated with views on social issues, such as support for diverse cultures and communities and more egalitarian views on issues such as LGBTQ rights and same-sex marriage. People with more education also tend to be more global in their outlook.[25] It is perhaps inevitable that throughout the world some have grown concerned as these more progressive views on social issues have taken hold in recent years, especially among those with higher levels of education. This shift threatens what they view as society's more "traditional" values and norms and is behind much of the appeal of authoritarianism.

For most of the history of the United States, public education has been understood to encourage tolerance among students, advance political participation, and support the development of other key skills needed to sustain American democracy. It is now also responsible for conveying the technical skills that will be required of entry-level workers as they enter the workforce of the future. But these goals are ultimately complementary, not contradictory.[26]

Yes, we need to do more to specifically prepare people for citizenship. The best way to do this is to cultivate and deploy their lifetime abilities to do human work. As we've seen earlier in this book, human work demands a range of higher-level skills such as critical thinking, problem solving, effective communication, and ethical reasoning. These skills, and others like them, are precisely what is needed to cut through narrow viewpoints and misleading information to make sense of complex issues. Critical thinking, problem solving, and communication skills, along with ethical thinking and decision making, are no longer necessary just for those with better jobs that require higher-level thinking—they are now essential skills for citizenship.

The Essential Skills for Citizenship

Earlier in the book, I talked about critical thinking and why it's such an important skill for human work. At its core, critical thinking is essentially the ability to apply rational analysis

to issues and ideas before forming opinions or reaching conclusions. In other words, it means to not make snap judgments or
blindly accept the conclusions of others—however satisfying or
consistent with our own beliefs they may be. If ever there were a
citizenship skill that is essential in this era of simplistic analysis
and polarized thinking, it is critical thinking. Sadly, it seems to
be in shorter supply than is needed.

As the name implies, problem solving is another higher-level
thinking skill that is essential to citizenship as well as human
work. While the ability to solve problems depends a lot on
context and often requires specialized or technical knowledge,
certain core habits of mind can characterize all problem solvers. One is the ability to frame or define a problem in ways that
can lead to a solution, while another is to be able to design and
implement a strategy to resolve an issue or reach a goal. While
this skill is obviously of extreme importance in work, it is clear
how useful it is for life in a complex and changing society.

In human work settings, effective communication is an essential
skill because working with and for people lie at its heart, whether
as a member of a team working together on a project or communi-
cating with customers or clients. Communication is the lifeblood of
society as well, especially when its purpose is to foster understanding. Despite the cacophony of voices that defines public life today,
true communication has perhaps never been in shorter supply.

We should also consider the need for ethical thinking in both
human work and the greater society. Most people decry the perceived lack of ethical behavior on the part of politicians, business
and religious leaders, and even educators.[27] But the ability to
analyze issues and make decisions from a rigorous ethical stand-
point is a real skill that can be learned.[28]

Another skill that must be developed at scale is global literacy. The United States stands as a glaring example of the negative consequences of failing to do this in recent decades. When
young Americans are asked to find Afghanistan on a map, only
one in ten will be able to do so. Ask them which language has

the world's largest number of native speakers, and three of four will say English rather than Mandarin.[29] Even college graduates fall down on global literacy. While they do better on knowledge of basic geography, two-thirds don't know Indonesia is a majority-Muslim country and only 10% know Canada is the United States's largest trading partner.

These and other discouraging statistics point to two serious problems for nations like the United States. The first is that global literacy has become a critical priority in a world with increasingly permeable boundaries, an integrated global economy, and challenges requiring coordinated and coherent international responses. Such literacy has never been more critical for the United States as, more than ever, our nation's economy and security are connected to the actions and interests of others.

The second is that graduates of our education system are poorly prepared to succeed in a global environment. They lack an awareness of history, appreciation of the complexity of the biosphere, and understanding of economic trends and tensions. Too few possess critical skills such as competence in another language and a deep understanding of cultures. Above all, they lack an appreciation for the effects global issues have on individuals and the society.

The reasons for our deficit in global knowledge and skills are obvious. While many colleges refer to global learning in their mission statements, few require their students to meet explicit expectations for global learning. In the instances where they do, students may often meet the requirement simply by taking one or two courses from a list of options—none of which offers a comprehensive perspective on major international issues or concerns.

Until recently, American inattentiveness to the global environment had not been that costly. The size and relative geographical detachment of the United States allowed the country to rely on the expertise of a few well-educated public servants, scholars, and corporate leaders. But accelerating challenges in today's "flat world" make it clear that pockets of global literacy are no longer enough. To properly address challenges in health care, diplomacy, economics, and the environment, global proficiency must emerge as a broad educational priority.

To be clear, poor global literacy among college and university graduates also has very real economic consequences. Only one in twenty people in the world is American. While the United States's share of global economic output remains strong, that share is declining—and is almost sure to decline further unless American colleges and universities prepare their graduates to operate in a globally interconnected world.

If Americans are to make responsible and well-informed decisions about their political leadership and weigh in on policies that affect their lives, they must become far better educated in global matters. If they can't find Afghanistan or Iraq on a map, how will they evaluate proposals governing sustained U.S. involvement there? If they know nothing of the history or culture of Korea, how can they evaluate political leaders and candidate statements on North Korea? If they are unfamiliar with the economic and social systems that drive China, how can they understand the influence of Chinese industry or the effectiveness of international treaties to protect the global environment? Without a minimum level of global literacy, how do we expect to counteract those who blame crime and unemployment on refugees and immigrants?

As the movement to educate or train more people after high school grows, we must ensure that degrees reflect rigorous learning that includes these international competencies. Defining the competencies is one key task. Others are to identify and develop appropriate instructional methods and materials for teaching them and then to have them adopted by colleges and universities through the active involvement of faculty members, who are key to curricular quality and innovation.

In short, we must better prepare students as global citizens who have the essential citizenship skills to navigate our complex and dangerous world. It's not enough that a small, well-educated elite learn the citizenship skills on the assumption that they will lead the rest of us. That way of running a society no longer works. Rather, we need to assure that many more people reach the much higher levels of thinking that our complex society—and the demands of human work—require. The talent needed for human work is the same as what we need to escape the dangerous trajectory we are on in civil society, and just as developing the talent of people is the key response to the future of work, likewise developing talent is the key to citizenship in a healthy society.

Active Citizenship and Service

When I talk about citizenship, I'm not just talking about voting and having an opinion on consequential issues of the day, although that's plenty important. What is more pressing is the notion of active citizenship—a not-new idea that maintaining a strong democracy requires citizens to be engaged in their communities and society. In the U.S. context, the idea was captured by Benjamin Franklin's famously pithy response to those who asked him after the Constitutional Convention what sort of government the delegates had created: "A republic, if you can keep it."

To the Founders, there was no such thing as passive citizenship. French diplomat, historian, and scientist Alexis de Tocqueville understood that civic passivity undermines democracy, and described the problem like this:

> "I seek to trace the novel features under which despotism may appear in the world. The first thing that strikes the observation is an innumerable multitude of men, all equal and alike, incessantly endeavoring to procure the petty and paltry pleasures with which they glut their lives. Each of them, living apart, is as a stranger to the fate of all the rest; his children and his private friends constitute to him the whole of mankind. As for the rest of his fellow citizens, he is close to them, but he does not see them; he touches them, but he does not feel them; he exists only in himself and for himself alone; and if his kindred still remain to him, he may be said at any rate to have lost his country."

It's as if he were looking into our own time as technology provides ever-new ways for people to "live apart." Technology certainly constitutes a threat to democracy if ways are not found to engage people for the greater good. Active citizenship is service. This is the essence of the idea that human work must include the deep capacity to serve others over the course of a lifetime.

While smart machines are capable of many things we thought impossible not so long ago, the ability to express compassion for others and to gain satisfaction from acting on this compassion are not among them. They are, however, key to human work. As Shirley Sagawa, the founding managing director of the U.S. Corporation for National Service in the 1990s and a leader in the American national service movement over the last three decades, told me in a conversation not long ago, "Service gives us a chance to do all of the human, caring things that robots can't do."

The question is, what does this have to do with learning? As our world becomes ever more complex, the level of talent needed for active citizenship rises, just as it does for human work. Indeed, the two are inseparable—the knowledge and skills people need for human work are the same as for citizenship in today's complex, and diverse, society.

The knowledge of how to be an effective citizen and actively contribute to the betterment of society must be learned. One concrete way to develop those skills is through service learning—structured, formal service programs for students. While service learning in some form has been around for as long as there have been colleges and universities, we need new approaches that work for all of today's students and in all the settings in which they are learning. There is no singular point where someone "graduates" as a citizen. It is an iterative process of civic and service learning, community engagement, and democratic practice. People grow in their civic identities over the course of their entire lives.

Making service opportunities available to all would help to cement the idea that an individual's development as a citizen, as a learner, and as a worker can coexist and be mutually reinforcing. It's an idea that gained traction amid record unemployment the United States experienced immediately after the pandemic forced an economic shutdown.

Let's start with learners. As we move toward a system of universal learning, we should assure that service is a part of it. For all students, service should be part of the curriculum. In recent years, several nations have moved toward "service year" plans. France, under the leadership of President Emmanuel Macron, developed a new tiered plan that links a short-term civic learning and culture element with a formal service element of up to one year in critical national need areas. The French model envisions a month of mandatory service that then is linked into the deeper, voluntary experience focused specifically on advancing the civic culture.[30]

In the United Kingdom, Rory Stewart, a distinguished member of Parliament and candidate for prime minister in 2019 (who eventually lost to Boris Johnson), proposed a national service initiative closer to a universal model than others that have been advanced. The United Kingdom has considerable experience with national service models at a scale not achieved in many other parts of the world. The National Citizens' Service, focused on teen service efforts, enrolls approximately 100,000 mostly 16- and 17-year-olds per year, and the results of this work are consistently strong. Young people spend a month in the countryside learning skills and working on projects with their peers and later volunteer in related fields in their communities. The United Kingdom is achieving many of its targets for this program—these young people report higher levels of confidence than other people their age, and they feel closer and more integrated into their communities and their peers. Perhaps most importantly, the effects seem to follow them for years after the program has ended.[31]

Pete Buttigieg, who sought the Democratic presidential nomination in 2020, offered what may be the most aggressive of the American national service plans to date. His plan, built on the numerous other plans advanced by U.S. civic advocates post-9/11, proposed a major expansion of voluntary public service programs to attract 250,000 Americans in the near term, with the potential to grow to one million a year by 2026. By comparison, the Peace Corps has about 7,300 volunteers and trainees while AmeriCorps has about 75,000 members.

Buttigieg called for expanding existing national service organizations, including AmeriCorps and the Peace Corps, but interestingly, he added an important and timely new wrinkle to prior proposals by suggesting new programs that are aimed at dealing with the leading issues of the day, including combating climate change, treating mental health and addiction, and providing care for older people. Buttigieg's plan also would have prioritized volunteers from and into predominantly communities of color and rural areas. "We really want to talk about the threat to social cohesion that helps characterize this presidency but also just this era," said Buttigieg, who served as the mayor of South Bend, Indiana. "One thing we could do that would change that would be to make it—if not legally obligatory but certainly a social norm—that anybody after they're 18 spends a year in national service."

To be sure, major obstacles have tripped up these kinds of proposals over the years. One is the ongoing debate between mandatory service and voluntary service. Making service mandatory, especially when it is for an extended time (such as the yearlong proposals that have been advanced) seems unworkable from a political perspective. But shorter-term mandatory service, like the French model, tied to longer, more immersive voluntary experiences for many people, may just work.

Another hurdle to universal service is clearly cost, though the expense is not an insurmountable barrier. In the United Kingdom, the total price tag for the 100,000 teens serving is about £180 million. Given there are around 1.5 million 16- to 17-year-olds in that country, scaling the program up to reach all of them is not a trivial matter. Yet, by comparison, recent proposals from U.S. presidential candidates calling for the elimination of accumulated college debt—which may cost upwards of $50 billion—are even more daunting. Moreover, unlike these service plans, debt forgiveness essentially aims at fixing a problem in the rearview mirror—excessive borrowing that already has taken place. A proactive universal service initiative, aimed squarely at meeting the needs of human workers who seek meaning and fulfillment to complete their learning and earning experiences, seems a smart long-term bet.

But service is not and should not be limited to students, and formal universal service programs are not the only way to assure everyone can do meaningful work of service to society and their communities. Service should be seen as integral to the educational and work experiences of participants. It should not be a "bolt on" or one-time phenomenon. Just as service should be part of education programs for its learning value and should count as such, workers should be able to serve during paid work time because employers will share the value of the enhanced skills learned through the experience.

All workers should have opportunities, offered by employers, for direct community engagement and volunteering. Workers should be able to do more service, not as an expectation of their jobs, but as a shared responsibility contract between each worker and employer. Both should understand the benefits of service and be able to recognize the "double bottom line" potential of these opportunities.

According to the National Council for Voluntary Organisations, a U.K.-based charitable group that champions volunteering and the voluntary sector "because they're essential for a better society," the opportunities for expansion of these types of efforts is significant. Both workers and employers rate these opportunities as highly successful and satisfying, but data show in the United Kingdom, as elsewhere, there are simply not enough of these service partnerships in place to meet worker demand. The council even touts the growing opportunities for digital or online service that lend themselves to online and off-line strategies. In one illustration, the council notes that a hospital that had been hacked by ransomware pirates was quickly brought back to operating status by a cadre of volunteer tech wizards from local companies. As then–council chair Peter Kellner said, "Welcome to 21st century volunteering."[32]

A year of national service, preferably early in life, would be a down payment on a lifetime of serving through human work. Tied to other employer-sponsored volunteer initiatives, and the collaborative efforts of nonprofits and other groups, the notion of universal service could achieve real scale.

Serving Others Is Integral to Human Work

As I talk about creating large-scale programs that give everyone the opportunity for service, I don't want us to forget that ser-vice is really about personal connections between individuals. Therein lies its power.

Earlier in the book, I told the success story of Herman Felton Jr., president of Wiley College. His journey from a housing project in Jacksonville, Florida, to the presidency of two historically black colleges is inspiring enough. But when he tells the story, he emphasizes something important: it never would have happened without pioneers and mentors who paved the way.

"Poverty was probably the biggest mentor, and my mom," he said. "Her work ethic—she was 17 when I was born and working two jobs as a janitor, six days a week. I don't remember her taking a day off." This work ethic "helped us navigate the perils of inner-city poverty."

There were others. Felton can't remember the name of the tutor who diagnosed his dyslexia when he was in the U.S. Marines studying for his GED after he had enlisted without a high school diploma. But he owes her a great debt, as she worked with him with flash cards to help him read about his favorite subject, history. And when he came out of the Marines and enrolled in Edward Waters College, he watched the college's president, Jimmy Jenkins, fight the board of trustees when they considered reducing the number of students who could be admitted under the open-door policy that made it possible for him to attend. "I just watched, and it didn't really resonate with me what really was at stake, meaning people like me not having an opportunity, until my president got up and annihilated them in a very powerful and passionate way," he said.

Felton went to law school at the University of Florida as a Virgil Hawkins scholar. The award helped him pay for law school, but it means something more to Felton. In 1949, Virgil Hawkins was denied admission to Florida's law school because of his race. He kept fighting for admission but chose to withdraw his application in 1958 in exchange for a Florida Supreme Court order desegregating the university's graduate and professional schools. After leaving the state to get a law degree, he was denied admission to the Florida bar. It was not until 1977, at the age of 69, that Hawkins was finally able to open his law practice in Florida.[33] "He kneeled so that we could stand," Felton said, adding that Hawkins's history "forever ingrained in my brain the true notion of sacrifice, what it really means to stand on principle, be it popular or not."

Felton knows he's been fortunate, and he wants to create new opportunities for college administrators who want to follow in his path. He and others established the Higher Education Leadership Foundation in 2015 to train young administrators to become future leaders of Historically Black Colleges and Universities (HBCUs). To date, five graduates of the academy have become presidents of HBCUs. Another fifteen have become provosts. Felton is committed to helping HBCUs, and he will spend the rest of his career in private HBCUs, forgoing opportunities in the larger public colleges that are historically black. He said he's found his mission, thanks to a lot of mentors along the way.

"I was given access to people who could change my life, and now I want to be that person for others," he said. "There is nothing more rewarding than unconditional giving."

All this shows the power of one kind of service—mentorship—and how it changes lives. Mentorship programs are an excellent example of the kind of service that should be expanded until everyone can have a mentor—and be one. Felton doesn't mention it, but I strongly suspect his mentors would say they, too, benefited—whether by learning from his experiences in our education systems or by inspiring them in their own work. From my perspective, service is the essential ingredient that combines with earning and learning to create the virtuous cycle of human work.

Improving global literacy, advancing civic knowledge and commitment through formal learning, and creating wholly new universal service opportunities at a national level represent a new, coordinated effort to enhance democracy through human work. This is the essence of the new age of human work, and the dawning of this new age will mark a watershed moment in the development of human potential to do work that makes a difference—work only humans can do in our world of blended existence between humans and smart machines.

Conclusion

Do all the good you can,
By all the means you can,
In all the ways you can,
In all the places you can,
At all the times you can,
To all the people you can,
As long as ever you can.
    —John Wesley, founder of Methodism, 1703–1791

It's no wonder the topic of work in the coming decades has captured the imagination of both pundits and the public. The changes that already have occurred in work and the economy are unprecedented in contemporary times and have affected everyone directly or indirectly. While some doubtless yearn for the return of the largely imagined good old days of high-paying factory jobs and the like, I believe few people really expect this to happen. Indeed, it seems many people around the world believe today's environment for jobs is not just a "new normal" but a way station to even more dramatic changes. What drives so much of our politics today is not so much nostalgia as anxiety about the future.

To be sure, much of that anxiety is about fundamental questions of work and life. What will I do in the future? How will I get along in the new, technology-enabled world of human-machine coexistence?

These questions are not easily answerable. Which and how many jobs will be lost or gained, how economic changes will affect different communities and regions, and who will benefit or lose from the new opportunities that the new world of work poses is yet to be determined. Will our future include even more unfairness by race, income, immigration status, gender, and other factors than the unacceptable levels we already have? And if so, what will happen to our society as a result? Will large segments of the population be cut off from meaningful participation in the economy, and if so, what will the lives of those people look like? The fact is, I don't know, and neither does anyone else.

But trying to predict what will happen is not really a constructive exercise. What matters is understanding what the changes in work are telling us about what we need to do to help everyone have a secure and rewarding future in tomorrow's economy. And what the trends in work are telling us is simple but profound in its implications.

1. Work brings meaning to our lives.

We're so used to thinking about work as something that employers *provide* but too often fail to realize work is what people *do*. This is even more true of the work of the future—human work that draws from the unique knowledge, skills, and abilities only humans have and can bring to tasks worth doing.

2. Human work is learning and serving as well as earning.

Work is how we expend our energies and interests to accomplish something of value. Sure, some work is paid and is therefore a job, but work and a job are not the same thing. Of course, we need to *earn* to provide for ourselves and those we care about. While it's often hard work, we also *learn* throughout our lives because learning is how we develop our knowledge, skills, and abilities and make sense of things. Human work requires wide learning—the idea that the learning element of human work includes the dimensions of time, people, and content. This notion is connected closely to the other work we do that is uniquely human, which is to *serve* others. We serve others by applying those energies and interests to make our communities and the world better. Earning, learning, and serving make up human work. They are equally important, they happen together, and everyone must have the opportunity to do them.

3. *As AI and other technologies automate repetitive tasks in all jobs, human work becomes less about specialized expertise in one task or set of tasks.*

Human work is emerging in four distinct kinds of work, which I have described as the work performed by Helpers, Bridgers, Integrators, and Creators. Helpers are engaged in occupations that involve deep personal interactions with people. In today's service economy, these jobs are everywhere as many industries have transformed to become focused on customers. Bridgers work in occupations that involve the interface between people and technical tasks and systems. Bridgers literally create connections—to other people, and to other forms of work. Integrators work in occupations that involve the integration of knowledge and skills from a range of fields and applying it in a highly personal way. Social workers and elementary school teachers are prime examples. These workers can also be people who apply the lessons learned in one context, perhaps over the course of many years, to extend those lessons into new or different fields. And Creators work in occupations that involve both highly technical skills and pure creativity. Whether one is a Helper, Bridger, Integrator, or Creator, human work draws upon the fullest possible range of human knowledge, skills, and abilities.

4. *Human work requires fundamental changes in our systems for earning, learning, and serving.*

Because work is central to the quality of our lives and society, we must assure everyone is prepared for and has opportunities to do human work—the work only humans can do. The work of today is often framed from the perspectives of the providers of work—whom they employ, for what purposes, and how much output they can generate from workers. Human work forces us to focus on the individual. After all, earning, learning, and serving is what individuals do—not what employers, schools, or society provide. But how do we assure everyone has the opportunity and ability to earn, learn, and serve? And how do we make sure human work reduces inequities by race, income, and other factors, rather than increasing those inequities? To make it possible for everyone to do human work, we will have to change many if not most of the structures around employment, education, and even community service that we are accustomed to and take for granted.

So how do we make this real? It turns out we know a lot more than we think about how to make all these changes. Everyone has a role to play, whether as employer, educator, policymaker, independent foundation, or worker.

1. Employers.

In the future of human work, employment and employers still matter—a lot. But they need to realize, as I believe many already do, they are no longer the definers of work—assuming they ever really were. For better or worse, the relationship between employers and workers has fundamentally changed. An incredible array of conditional work arrangements has arisen, and even more workers in the future will have only temporary connections with whoever is employing them. Even more important is that employers need to understand the future of their enterprises, whatever they do and however they organize their work, will rely on workers doing human work.

Employers must embrace and reflect the diversity of their employees, their customers or clients, and their communities. They must recognize changing demographics represent more than a new challenge. They represent an opportunity to accomplish their objectives more effectively and more completely by ensuring everyone they encounter is fully engaged and not marginalized—especially in these times of renewed animus and conflict globally aimed at immigrants, people of color, and women.

Employers need to take charge of this future and step up to make it work for them and their workers. They can begin by defining transparently exactly what they need in terms of the knowledge, skills, and abilities that workers should have. But it doesn't stop there. Employers must have strategies to attract and retain talent, and they need to assure that their workers can fully develop their talents throughout their career and life, whatever the structure of their work relationship. Continuous learning is an integral part of the work of the future, and employers need to assure everyone has the opportunity for it.

Human work also includes deep and meaningful service to others, and employers have a responsibility to make sure people can serve while they earn. Yes, every workplace should provide opportunities to do service in the community. But beyond that, the value of the enterprise to the community and greater society should be uppermost in both long-term and day-to-day decision making. Workers should feel that their work is of value not just to employers, but to the broader society.

2. Educators.

In the future of human work, educators matter even more than they do today. But everyone—not just a fortunate few—must have the opportunity to develop their knowledge, skills, and abilities for human work. This should be great news for educators and our education systems, but instead it represents one of the greatest challenges they will ever face. To meet this urgent need, educators will need to question almost all the assumptions that have guided the development of our current systems.

For starters, educators at all levels must focus on the success of *all* their students. Particularly in higher education, this represents a big change—and not just in the obvious way of professors never again saying, "Look left and look right; one of you will be gone by the end of the semester." While it's true that some still have the outdated attitude that students are solely responsible for their own success or failure, that's never been what most educators believe. We all have a stake in the success of today's students, because those increasingly diverse students—those who represent the nation's fastest-growing racial and ethnic groups, those who are older or immigrants, and many others—are the human workers of tomorrow.

Focusing a college or university on student success changes it in fundamental ways. Fortunately, plenty of institutions are showing the way, and success rates are increasing. But all educators must embrace the student success agenda and make it their own.

Another big challenge for educators is that what students learn, and not just whether they show up in class or finish a program of studies, should be the main goal. Educators care about student learning, but that's not enough. What students learn—what they know and can do at the end of a course or program—must be clear and demonstrable to everyone. Yes, students require content knowledge in key areas, from mathematics and science to the arts and literature. But they also must be equipped with learning that enhances their human traits such as compassion, empathy, and ethics. They need the broad range of skills demanded by human work. They must also be deeply imbued with values that reflect the democratic and civic virtues of a modern world riven by conflict, misinformation, and technology-fueled discord.

All of this requires use of the new tools that are becoming available to educators and others, including skills frameworks, transparent credentials, learning passports, and many more. All these tools offer educators ways to improve what really matters— the learning of students and the benefits they derive from their education.

3. Policymakers.

Given my two decades of experience leading public policy research, I often see the world through the lens of effective public policy aimed at improving the human condition. While that worldview has not changed, it is not what has primarily animated my thinking on this topic of human work, as evidenced by the lack of policy proposals in this book. Still, public policy matters—a lot—in building the system that meets people's needs for human work and prepares them for it. This includes explicitly and directly addressing the racial and other equity challenges that prevent people from achieving their full potential. A good place to start is to rethink all the government incentives that employers, educators, and workers operate under to make them work in a world of human work.

All types of public policy, including tax policy, need to offer employers and workers the incentive to invest in developing the knowledge, skills, and abilities needed for human work. We provide incentives to businesses to invest in technology that replaces humans. So why can't we give them more of an incentive to develop their workers' abilities for human work?

Similarly, government policies, including funding approaches, that treat education and training as separate activities performed by different systems are obsolete and need to be scrapped. I can scarcely imagine the infighting and turf wars this shift in policy will cause, but that's no reason for policymakers to shy away from it. The needs are too urgent, and the potential to better serve many more people is too great.

And policymakers must push back against the authoritarian and antidemocratic tendencies of the current crop of global leaders. Their authoritarian views are dangerous to democracy, pluralism, and the thriving of human workers in this new machine-enabled era.

4. Philanthropy.

Because I run a large national foundation committed to making opportunities for learning beyond high school available to all, I see an important role for the social sector in this new human work era. The reason is not merely that we have financial resources that can be deployed to support this work. The uniqueness of philanthropy's role lies elsewhere. In the kinds of philanthropy Lumina Foundation and many other foundations practice, we have a capacity to lead the way in influencing and supporting systemic change that other institutions lack.[1]

Foundations have three attributes that are potential strengths in addressing big issues like the future of human work. The first is that they have a unique ability to take risks. Risk is necessary to true innovation. Policymakers, for example, may well be aware of the need for fundamentally different approaches to human work, but they can also be constrained from acting by the political consequences if a new approach doesn't work. While foundations can support a range of approaches as part of strategies to find effective solutions, policymakers seldom have this luxury.

The second is foundations can take a longer view of change while other actors are constrained by the need to seek more immediate results. For example, however much they may want to, organizations that operate on annual budget cycles may be unable to invest in building new capacities to serve human workers that will pay off in the long term.

And the third important attribute of foundations is that they can engage all the myriad actors who must be involved in responding to the demands of human work. This is where foundations' inability to directly affect systemic change, on their own, is an advantage. The endowments of foundations, while large compared to the size of many other types of organizations, are dwarfed in comparison to the budgets of governments, or the market valuations of large companies. Through strategies such as exercising thought leadership, convening experts, and coalition building, foundations can instead create the environments in which different constituencies can act in concert to build the new human work ecosystem the future will demand.

But with these advantages comes the responsibility for foundations to be transparent about their worldviews and objectives. Lumina Foundation, as well as other funders focused on education, workforce development, and human flourishing, should view their strategies through the lens of preparing people for human work. Our efforts to date have been focused on the worthy objective of expanding opportunity by addressing disparities affecting marginalized people. Going forward, we should also be prepared to better answer the question, *What are we preparing them for?* This means foundations should invest in new strategies to understand human work needs and develop tools and capacities that ready everyone for the virtuous cycle of learning, earning, and serving.

5. Workers.

What workers need to do is the key to everything else that needs to happen to prepare us for a future of human work. Of course, workers must understand the need to develop their knowledge, skills, and abilities for human work throughout their lives and careers. But I don't believe that's a big problem. I believe workers *want* to do so—have an innate *drive* to do so—and we need to offer them a system that gets out of their way and lets them do so.

Workers need to own their learning in the same way people now need to own their health. What I mean by this is that workers must know not just the credentials they have earned and how to obtain their transcripts. They need to know what they *know* and can *do* clearly enough to describe it to current and potential employers. With this knowledge, workers need to think strategically about how they will develop their abilities through continual learning and seek out opportunities—including employment opportunities—that will allow them to build on what they know and can do.

But there is another inescapable truth about the future of human work that workers need to understand. Human work includes an interconnected combination of earning, learning, and serving—and workers need to do all three. Workers need to understand that work is not just about "making a living" but includes everything we apply our talents and energy to and that helps bring meaning to our lives. Of course, this has always been true—it's just that the future of human work makes that clear once again to all of us.

The Future of Work Is Human Work

This brings us back to the beginning. It's easy to get caught up in the hype about the "future of work" and the dramatic and unprecedented ways AI and other technologies will change our economy and society. It's not all hype—the changes so far have been extensive, and it's likely even bigger changes are in store.

But as I've examined the implications of the work of the future for all of us, I've seen that rather than representing the end of work, the work of the future will be human work—work that draws on our unique abilities. Our challenge as a society is not to find ways to support and entertain people without jobs. The challenge instead is to assure *everyone* can do human work and has the opportunity to develop the knowledge, skills, and abilities needed for it.

I am struck that many of the innovative solutions we will turn to in meeting this challenge look like throwbacks to an earlier age—apprenticeships, demonstrated mastery, even guilds. Likewise, the kind of life human work allows us to lead sounds curiously old-fashioned. It's a life of meaningful work, continuous learning, and service to community. Perhaps the effects of AI and technology on the work of the future is less a leap forward into the unknown as a return from industrial-age ways of organizing the economy and society to something more personal and individual. After all, what's left after the smart machines take over whatever they can do is human intelligence, drive, and values.

We have learned that the introduction of technology to an industrial economy leads to increases in the inherent inequity or unfairness, which is hovering at unacceptable levels and, if left unchecked, will bring our global society and economy crashing down. Already today, far too many people are cut off from full participation in the economy and society because of their race, ethnicity, gender, immigration status, and other factors. A future of human work offers us a chance to change this, but only if we are willing to confront the issue of fairness. Our great challenge is to give all people—and I do mean *all people*—the chance to do human work, including preparing for it by developing their unique abilities.

The disproportionate effects of the COVID-19 pandemic on Americans who are black and brown has brought with it staggering levels of unemployment on top of a foundation of injustice. These social and economic conditions have had devastating consequences for the fabric of the entire nation, affecting all of us as Americans.

None of this is a coincidence. These grim conditions arise from unfair policies, actions, beliefs, and assumptions over hundreds of years specifically designed to disadvantage people of color—and over time from stark leadership failures. Policies, practices, and beliefs—rooted in history and still affecting people today—keep many black, Native American, and Latino people from the education and skills they need and desire.

The demonstrations, protests, and marches following the death of George Floyd at the hands of Minneapolis police mean all of us must sharpen our focus on fixing systems that unfairly hold people back. We must remove barriers and obstacles so we can better prepare people for informed, active citizenship and to contribute to our collective success in a global economy.

The COVID-19 pandemic makes it impossible to ignore the injustice and inequity facing vulnerable groups in society—including people of color, the poor, and immigrants and refugees. Many of them lost low-skilled jobs that smart machines eventually will recast as human work.

We cannot afford to be naive about the challenges we face. The rise in authoritarianism across the globe is itself a reaction to the creation of a more just and open economy and society, and the powerful forces that want to maintain privilege based on un-earned advantages will not be easily overcome. Here, again, the only true antidote to the seduction of authoritarianism is to develop people's full potential and assure they have the opportunity to contribute in meaningful ways through human work.

Seen in this context, service is not just a nice thing to do for those with the time and resources but an essential component of a meaningful life. Service is a form of human work—perhaps the most human work there is—and everyone should have the opportunity to do human work that makes a difference in their communities and the greater society.

Whether the approaches are innovative or time-honored, we know what we need to do to create an economy and society built around human work. We must build a new learning system in which education and work are integrated in ways that offer everyone the opportunity to fully develop their talents. Our entire system of employment must be restructured around the talent of people, including full transparency regarding the knowledge, skills, and abilities that jobs require. We must create new approaches that offer people the opportunity to use their talents in service of their communities and the society. We must have the courage to act even though we know most of our treasured institutions and approaches will need to change and the people within them will have to adapt.

As always, we will hear cries that doing what needs to be done is impossible, that it will undermine educational quality, that it will destroy what has taken years to build. But far too many people across the globe today are trapped in vicious cycles of hopelessness. Rather than moving forward economically for themselves and their families, their lack of knowledge, skills, and abilities for human work limits whatever opportunities they might have to escape dead-end jobs or even poverty. Our existing education and training systems don't offer most of them any meaningful chance to obtain what they need to be equipped for human work. Too often, they feel a sense of isolation—as if the world is moving on without them—which leaves them disengaged from making their communities better places to live.

It doesn't have to be this way. The future of human work could create a virtuous cycle of earning, learning, and serving that opens opportunity to many people who are now excluded.

Believing in people and human work is the right way forward—indeed, it's the only way. A world in which everyone has the chance to earn, learn, and serve by doing meaningful work is a world worth fighting for.

Acknowledgments

It's no exaggeration to say that this book would not have been possible without the diligence, expertise, and collegiality of two key people: Dewayne Matthews and Doug Richardson. Dewayne and I have a long history together that preceded my arrival at Lumina Foundation in 2008, continued when we overlapped as Lumina colleagues, and has endured since his retirement from the Foundation in 2017. Dewayne wrote, edited, and brainstormed with me over the course of the fifteen months or so that it took to craft this book. I'm deeply grateful for his support and friendship. And Doug collaborated in this work; he did the reporting on the majority of the human stories that are the backbone of the book. As an experienced journalist and gifted storyteller, Doug was able to source, research, and bring to life many of the stories that I offer as illustrations of the new human work paradigm. The complexity of human work is not easy to capture on a book jacket, and for that reason I'm deeply appreciative of Sarah Herbert's artistic vision. And many thanks to Rob Friedman for invaluable speech writing counsel.

I'm also grateful to my Lumina Foundation colleagues, including our amazingly talented Board of Directors and staff, for their encouragement and support in writing this book. The Board gave me the time and space to begin work on the book during a sabbatical I took with family in London during the first half of 2019, and I returned with an enthusiasm and focus on our work that made this book possible. Special thanks to my Lumina colleagues Chauncy Lennon, Debra Humphreys, Kevin Corcoran, Dave Powell, and John Strauss for reviewing and commenting on drafts of the book, and to Brad Kelsheimer, Courtney Brown, Danette Howard, and Holly McKiernan for feedback and suggestions that have deeply influenced my thinking. While the book is my own work and not a statement of Foundation goals or priorities, ultimately my hope is that it will serve as an ideas bank that can be drawn upon from over time as needed to inform Lumina's future work.

Anthony Carnevale and Ken Goldberg deserve special mention both for the contribution of specific ideas and data that I have liberally used in this book, and for their useful feedback on the manuscript draft.

The people who were interviewed for the personal stories and organizational profiles, or who served as expert commentators, were generous with their time and candor in helping me tell these stories in a way that is authentic. Sincere thanks to Katie Albright, Russell Lowery-Hart, Herman J. Felton Jr., Katherine Bush Felton, Penny Pritzker, Marcus Dodson, Richard Perko, Jody Wood, Paul Helmke, Rodney Owens, Eric Easton, Marcia McCallum, Nicholas Kwiatkowski, Andreas Thurner, Mark Sciarra, Jim Wolford, Linus Onuoha, De'Angelo Parker, Erich Mische, Majd Sekkar, Anne Greenwood, John Hlinko, Elizabeth Hoegeman, Jon Mills, Jordan Anderson, Joel Lewis, Jim Plump, Jaquan Gordon, Teresa Riggins Smith, Trish Holliday, and Malaika White.

Several people offered counsel, general advice, and contacts to help put the human face on human work. Thank you to Joseph Fuller, Shirley Sagawa, Mark Emkes, and Burns Phillips for this important support. Thanks also to Jeff Strohl and Holly Zanville for leads on people or important information that helped provide context for my arguments.

Thanks to the team at RosettaBooks and Simon & Schuster for the professionalism and enthusiasm shown to publish this book and get it into the hands of those who can do some good with these ideas. I'm grateful especially to Arthur Klebanoff for taking a second shot with me on this book, and to Brian Skulnik and Michelle Weyenberg for a terrific team effort. I am also grateful to Leah Paulos and her team at Press Shop PR, including Andy Davis, Brianne Kane, Liv Walton, and Emma McGlashen, who—along with Tracy Chen and Kate Snedeker—tirelessly spread the word about this book by pitching interviews to journalists, bloggers, and podcasters across the country. Lumina's live events team, led by Dominique Raymond, helped me share the ideas in this book. I also truly appreciate Pubvendo's digital marketing team, led by Joshua and Brandon Schwartz and Ashley Durrer, which helped us reach an even larger audience.

My family continues to be a great source of inspiration and is the best and most authentic focus group I could ask for when it comes to testing the soundness of my ideas. Thank you to my amazing spouse and editor, Colleen O'Brien, and our children, Elizabeth Merisotis and Benjamin Merisotis, for reminding me every day that the most important part of human work is the people themselves.

Notes

Prologue

1 Pope John Paul II, "*Laborem Exercens*," Encyclical, September 1981. http://www.vatican.va/content/john-paul-ii/en/encyclicals/documents/hf_jp-ii_enc_14091981_laborem-exercens.html
2 This quote has been attributed to numerous people, from Frank Zappa to Laurie Anderson to Martin Mull.
3 Roy Bahat and Bryn Freedman, "How do we find meaning at work?" TED Talks, November 2018. https://www.ted.com/talks/roy_bahat_and_bryn_freedman_what_is_the_meaning_of_work/transcript
4 Tom Peters, *The Excellence Dividend*, Vintage, 2018.

Chapter 1

1 "Ruth Bader Ginsberg: Rejected by the firm," Makers.com interview, June 2012. https://www.youtube.com/watch?v=ldFUmU-OZ1U
2 Bernard Marr, "The Future of Work: Are you ready for smart cobots?," *Forbes*, August 29, 2018. https://www.forbes.com/sites/bernardmarr/2018/08/29/the-future-of-work-are-you-ready-for-smart-cobots/#6ce40888522b
3 A Google search for "future of work" yields about 125,000,000 results.
4 Leonhard Teichert, "The Impact of AI on the Future of Work: A Philosophical Approach (Part I)," *Medium*, September 13, 2018. https://medium.com/hivedata/the-impact-of-ai-on-the-future-of-work-a-philosophical-approach-part-i-e5aff3bb0a30
5 "Proof emerges that a quantum computer can outperform a classical one," *The Economist*, September 26, 2019. https://www.economist.com/science-and-technology/2019/09/26/proof-emerges-that-a-quantum-computer-can-outperform-a-classical-one

6 Klaus Schwab, "The Fourth Industrial Revolution," World Economic Forum, January 3, 2017.

7 Randall Hill, "Half of all U.S. jobs eliminated," rchp.com. http://business.rchp.com/home-2/half-of-all-jobs-eliminated/

8 Oliver Griffin, "How artificial intelligence will impact accounting," *ICAEW*, October 6, 2019. https://economia.icaew.com/features/october-2016/how-artificial-intelligence-will-impact-accounting

9 James Vincent, "Automation threatens 800 million jobs, but technology could still save us, says report," *The Verge*, November 30, 2017. https://www.theverge.com/2017/11/30/16719092/automation-robots-jobs-global-800-million-forecast

10 Calum McClelland, "The Impact of Artificial Intelligence—Widespread Job Losses," *IoT For All*, January 15, 2020. https://www.iotforall.com/impact-of-artificial-intelligence-job-losses/. Even those who believe 99% of current jobs will be eliminated do not see a future without work.

11 "CGI could leave actors out of a job," *BBC News*, December 15, 2013. https://www.bbc.com/news/av/entertainment-arts-25388672/cgi-could-leave-actors-out-of-a-job-freeman

12 Andy Beckett, "Post-work: the radical idea of a world without jobs," *The Guardian*, January 19, 2018. https://www.theguardian.com/news/2018/jan/19/post-work-the-radical-idea-of-a-world-without-jobs

13 Erin Winick, "Every study we could find on what automation will do to jobs, in one chart," *MIT Technology Review*, January 25, 2018. https://www.technologyreview.com/s/610005/every-study-we-could-find-on-what-automation-will-do-to-jobs-in-one-chart/

14 Carl Benedikt Frey and Michael A. Osborne, "The Future of Employment: How susceptible are jobs to computerisation?" Oxford Martin Programme on Technology and Employment, September 2013.

15 Susan Lund and James Manyika, "Five lessons from history on AI, automation, and employment," McKinsey Global Institute, November 28, 2017. https://www.mckinsey.com/featured-insights/future-of-work/five-lessons-from-history-on-ai-automation-and-employment#

16 Siobhan Wagner and Shelly Hagan, "Finance Needs People Who Work Well With Robots," *Bloomberg*, August 20, 2019. https://www.bloomberg.com/news/articles/2019-08-20/finance-needs-people-who-work-well-with-robots

17 "Will AI Replace the Majority of Jobs in Finance by 2030?" *The Motley Fool*, October 14, 2019. https://www.fool.ca/2019/10/14/will-ai-replace-the-majority-of-jobs-in-finance-by-2030/

18 Julia Sklar, "Robots Lay Three Times as Many Bricks as Construction Workers," *MIT Technology Review*, September 2, 2015. https://www.technologyreview.com/s/540916/robots-lay-three-times-as-many-bricks-as-construction-workers/

19 Quoctrung Bui and Roger Kisby, "Bricklayers Think They're Safe From Robots. Decide for Yourself." *The New York Times*, March 6, 2018.

https://www.nytimes.com/interactive/2018/03/07/upshot/bricklayers-think-theyre-safe-from-automation-robots.html

20 "Megatrends: The future of work," Vanguard Research, 2018.

21 Richard Baldwin, *The Globotics Upheaval: Globalization, Robotics and the Future of Work*, Oxford University Press, 2019.

22 Jonathan Rothwell and Steve Crabtree, "Not Just a Job: New Evidence on the Quality of Work in the United States," Gallup, 2019.

23 Lumina Foundation, "I always felt I had the potential to do more," *Focus,* Fall 2017, 20–23.

24 "The State of American Jobs," Pew Research Center, October 6, 2016. Using 2008 as a baseline, the number of jobs requiring an above-average level of skills increased twice as fast as those requiring a below-average level of skills.

25 "America's Divided Recovery," Georgetown University Center on Education and the Workforce, 2019.

26 OECD, OECD Employment Outlook 2018, OECD Publishing, 2018. https://read.oecd-ilibrary.org/employment/oecd-employment-outlook-2018_empl_outlook-2018-en#page1

27 "Skills Matter: Further Results from the Survey of Adult Skills," OECD, 2016. The U.S. is right at the OECD average on this measure.

28 Richard Vedder and Justin Strehle, "The Diminishing Returns of a College Degree," *The Wall Street Journal*, June 4, 2017. This article cites the fact that the wage premium for four-year college graduates fell from $32,900 in 2000 to $29,867 in 2015—after rising from $19,776 in 1975—as evidence of oversupply, and then asked the rhetorical question "Is it possible that by 2030 a master's degree in janitorial science could be a prerequisite for a job sweeping floors?"

29 "Facing the Future: U.S., U.K. and Canadian citizens call for a unified skills strategy for the AI age," Northeastern University and Gallup Inc., 2019.

30 Caroline Hill, "Deloitte Insight: Over 100,000 legal roles to be automated," *Legal IT Insider*, March 16, 2016. https://www.legaltechnology.com/latest-news/deloitte-insight-100000-legal-roles-to-be-automated/

31 Oliver Griffin, "How artificial intelligence will impact accounting," *ICAEW*, October 6, 2016. https://economia.icaew.com/features/october-2016/how-artificial-intelligence-will-impact-accounting

32 James Manyika, Susan Lund, Michael Chui, Jacques Bughin, Jonathan Woetzel, Parul Batra, Ryan Ko, and Saurabh Sanghvi, "Jobs lost, jobs gained: What the future of work will mean for jobs, skills, and wages," McKinsey Global Institute, November 28, 2017.

33 "Facing the Future: U.S., U.K. and Canadian citizens call for a unified skills strategy for the AI age," Northeastern University and Gallup Inc., 2019.

34 "Independent Work: Choice, Necessity, and the Gig Economy," McKinsey Global Institute, October 2016.

35 OECD, The Future of Work: OECD Employment Outlook 2019, http://www.oecd.org/employment/Employment-Outlook-2019-Highlight-EN.pdf

36 "The Global Learner Survey," Pearson, September 2019.

37 "Investing in People: A Strategy to Address America's Workforce Crisis," *Background Papers, Volume II*, U.S. Commission on Workforce Quality and Labor Market Efficiency, 1989, pp. 1521–1557.

38 Roger L. Martin, "The Rise (and Likely Fall) of the Talent Economy," *Harvard Business Review*, October 2014. https://hbr.org/2014/10/the-rise-and-likely-fall-of-the-talent-economy

39 Michael Kearns and Jon Younger, "The End of Traditional Employment—The Other Gig Economy," *Toptal*, https://www.toptal.com/insights/future-of-work/traditional-employment-gig-economy

40 Jordan Yadoo, "Six-Figure Earners Are a Growing Share of U.S. 'Gig' Workforce," *Bloomberg*, June 13, 2017. https://www.bloomberg.com/news/articles/2017-06-13/six-figure-earners-form-a-growing-share-of-u-s-gig-workforce

41 Anne Case and Angus Deaton, "Rising morbidity and mortality in midlife among white non-Hispanic Americans in the 21st century," Proceedings of the National Academy of Sciences (PNAS), December 8, 2015.

42 Anne Case and Sir Angus Deaton, "Mortality and Morbidity in the 21st Century," The Brookings Institution, March 23, 2017.

43 Arline T. Geronimus, John Bound, Timothy A. Waidmann, Javier M. Rodriguez, and Brenden Timpe, "Weathering, Drugs, and Whack-a-Mole: Fundamental and Proximate Causes of Widening Educational Inequity in U.S. Life Expectancy by Sex and Race, 1990–2015," *Journal of Health and Social Behavior,* June 13, 2019, 222–239.

44 Michael Batty, Jesse Bricker, Joseph Briggs, Elizabeth Holmquist, Susan McIntosh, Kevin Moore, Eric Nielsen, Sarah Reber, Molly Shatto, Kamila Sommer, Tom Sweeney, and Alice Henriques Volz, "Introducing the Distributional Financial Accounts of the United States," Finance and Economics Discussion Series 2019-017, Washington: Board of Governors of the Federal Reserve System, 2019. https://doi.org/10.17016/FEDS.2019.017

45 Harin Contractor and Spencer Overton, "An Introduction to the Future of Work in the Black Rural South," Joint Center for Political and Economic Studies, 2019.

46 For analysis of the data regarding good jobs, see A.P. Carnevale, J. Strohl, N. Ridley, and A. Gulish, "Educational Pathways to Good Jobs: High School, Middle Skills, and Bachelor's Degree," Georgetown University Center on Education and the Workforce, 2018; and J. Schmitt and J. Jones, "Making Jobs Good," Center for Economic and Policy Research, April 2013.

47 "Not Just Any Old Job: New Evidence on the Quality of Work in the United States," Gallup, unpublished manuscript, 2019.

48 "Facing the Future: U.S., U.K. and Canadian citizens call for a unified skills strategy for the AI age," Northeastern University and Gallup Inc., 2019.

49 Ryan Avent, *The Wealth of Humans: Work, Power, and Status in the Twenty-First Century*, St. Martin's Press, 2016.

50 Debra Humphreys and Paul Gaston, "Unlocking the Nation's Potential: A Model to Advance Quality and Equity in Education Beyond High School," Lumina Foundation, September 10, 2019. https://www.luminafoundation. org/resources/unlocking-the-nations-potential

Chapter 2

1 PwC Banking 2020 Survey. In the U.S., enhancing customer service was the second-highest investment priority, following regulatory compliance.
2 "Patients' Perceptions of Quality in Healthcare," European Patients Forum, February 2017.
3 Lumina Foundation, "Grocery chain puts young workers on the path to success," *Focus*, Spring 2018, 2–11.
4 Robert J. Schiller, *Narrative Economics: How Stories Go Viral and Drive Major Economic Events*, Princeton University Press, October 2019.
5 James Batchelor, "The Year in Numbers 2018," GamesIndustry.biz, December 17, 2018. https://www.gamesindustry.biz/articles/2018-12-17-gamesindustry-biz-presents-the-year-in-numbers-2018
6 Entertainment Software Association, 2018.
7 Dan Kopf, "Almost all the U.S. jobs created since 2005 are temporary," *Quartz*, December 5, 2016. https://qz.com/851066/almost-all-the-10-million-jobs-created-since-2005-are-temporary/
8 "Independent work: Choice, necessity, and the gig economy," McKinsey Global Institute, October 2016. https://www.mckinsey.com/featured-insights/employment-and-growth/independent-work-choice-necessity-and-the-gig-economy
9 David Nordfors and Vint Cerf, *The People Centered Economy: The New Ecosystem For Work*, Amazon Digital Services LLC - Kdp Print Us, October 2018.
10 Feras A. Batarseh, "Thoughts on the future of human knowledge and machine intelligence," *LSE Business Review*, September 20, 2017. https://blogs.lse.ac.uk/businessreview/2017/09/20/thoughts-on-the-future-of-human-knowledge-and-machine-intelligence/
11 Marc Rosenberg, "Marc My Words: The Coming Knowledge Tsunami," *Learning Solutions*, October 10, 2017. https://learningsolutionsmag.com/articles/2468/marc-my-words-the-coming-knowledge-tsunami
12 David J. Deming and Kadeem L. Noray, "STEM Careers and the Changing Skill Requirements of Work," National Bureau of Economic Research, September 2018, revised June 2019.
13 He likens it to the complementarity of Spock and Kirk from *Star Trek*.
14 Benjamin S. Bloom, ed., *Taxonomy of Educational Objectives: The Classification of Educational Goals*, David McKay Company, 1956.
15 "Beyond Tech: The Rising Demand for IT Skills in Non-Tech Industries," Burning Glass Technologies and Oracle Academy, September 2019.

Chapter 3

1   Job Openings and Labor Turnover Survey, Bureau of Labor Statistics, March 15, 2019.

2   Global Learner Survey, Pearson, September 2019.

3   Marco Annunziata, "Manufacturing Skills Gap: Myth, or Real Threat to Competitiveness?" *Forbes*, February 20, 2019. https://www.forbes.com/sites/marcoannunziata/2019/02/20/skills-gap-myth-or-real-threat-to-competitiveness/#1510a12930e3

4   Alicia Sasser Modestino, Daniel Shoag, and Joshua Ballance, "Upskilling: Do Employers Demand Greater Skill When Workers Are Plentiful?" Federal Reserve Bank of Boston, Working Paper No. 14–17, January 30, 2015. https://www.aeaweb.org/conference/2019/preliminary/paper/yySyK7fd

5   Mick Warwicker, "Education for life, or for work?" *The Guardian*, July 25, 2011. https://www.theguardian.com/education/2011/jul/25/white-paper-universities-training-jobs

6   Ibid.

7   Ronald D'Amico and Peter Z. Schochet, "The Evaluation of the Trade Adjustment Assistance Program: A Synthesis of Major Findings," *Mathematica Policy Research Reports*, December 2012. https://wdr.doleta.gov/research/FullText_Documents/ETAOP_2013_08.pdf

8   It has been called the Workforce Innovation and Opportunity Act (WIOA) since 2015, and the Workforce Investment Act (WIA) before that.

9   Katie Spiker, "Despite focus from the administration, budget falls short on much needed investment in workforce and education programs," National Skills Coalition, March 12, 2019. https://www.nationalskillscoalition.org/news/blog/despite-focus-from-the-administration-budget-falls-short-on-much-needed-investment-in-workforce-and-education-programs

10 Tamara Hiler and Lanae Erickson, "Beyond Free College and Free Markets: Voters Want Greater Accountability in Higher Ed," Third Way, June 17, 2019. https://www.thirdway.org/polling/beyond-free-college-and-free-markets-voters-want-greater-accountability-in-higher-ed

11 Ibid.

12 Rachel Fishman, "College Decisions Survey: Deciding to Go to College," New America, May 28, 2015. https://www.newamerica.org/education-policy/edcentral/collegedecisions/

13 Hiler and Erickson.

14 Digest of Education Statistics, National Institute for Education Statistics, 2019.

15 Demographic and Enrollment Characteristics of Nontraditional Undergraduates: 2011–12, National Center for Education Statistics, September 2015.

16 Alvin Powell, "Business School's Anand named vice provost for advances in learning," *The Harvard Gazette*, July 31, 2018. https://news.harvard.edu/gazette/story/2018/07/bharat-anand-to-take-over-as-harvards-vice-provost-for-advances-in-learning/

17 "VALUE: Valid Assessment of Learning in Undergraduate Education," Association of American Colleges and Universities, 2019. http://www.aacu. org/value/index.cfm

18 Michael Gardner, "Germany has leading position in tertiary STEM subjects," *University World News*, September 15, 2017. https://www. universityworldnews.com/post.php?story=20170915095958885

19 Science and Engineering Indicators 2014, National Science Board. https:// nsf.gov/statistics/seind14/

20 Deming and Noray.

21 Caroline Newman, "How time spent in an art museum can improve medical students' skills," *UVA Today,* November 14, 2019.https://news. virginia.edu/content/how-time-spent-art-museum-can-improve-medical-students-skills?utm_source=UVAThisMonth&utm_medium=email&utm_campaign=UVAThisMonth_11-19

22 "Profile Facts (2010 to Present)," Nashville State Community College. https:// s3.amazonaws.com/nscc.edu/PDFs/IR/Profile_Facts_2010_to_Present.pdf

23 Lumina Foundation, 2020.

24 Marc Zao-Sanders and Kelly Palmer, "Why Even New Grads Need to Reskill for the Future," *Harvard Business Review*, September 26, 2019. https://hbr.org/2019/09/why-even-new-grads-need-to-reskill-for-the-future

Chapter 4

1 "Marlon Brando quotes," Citatis. https://citatis.com/a10257/211a0e/

2 "Professional cloud architect," Google Cloud. https://cloud.google.com/ certification/cloud-architect

3 "Certified ScrumMaster," ScrumAlliance. https://www.scrumalliance.org/ get-certified/scrum-master-track/certified-scrummaster

4 "Cyber security certification programs," EC-Council. https://www. eccouncil.org/

5 Global Knowledge 2019 IT Skills and Salary Report.

6 Richard Arum and Josipa Roksa, *Academically Adrift: Limited Learning on College Campuses*, University of Chicago Press, 2011.

7 "Counting U.S. Postsecondary and Secondary Credentials—A 2019 report," Credential Engine, September 2019. https://credentialengine.org/ counting-credentials-2019-report/

8 "The Key Attributes Employers Seek on Students' Resumes," National Association of Colleges and Employers, November 30, 2017.

9 Gallup–Lumina Foundation Study on Higher Education, 2015. https:// www.gallup.com/topic/gallup_lumina.aspx

10 "Strategies for the New Economy: Skills as the Currency of the Labour Market," World Economic Forum, January 2019. https://www.weforum. org/whitepapers/strategies-for-the-new-economy-skills-as-the-currency-of-the-labour-market

11 "About Europass," Europass. https://europass.cedefop.europa.eu/about-europass

12 Lumina Foundation, "UW-Milwaukee 'Flex' program helps nursing students chart career success," *Focus*: "Real-life learning" Summer 2017, 33.

13 SkillsFuture homepage. https://www.skillsfuture.sg/

14 "About," Open Badges. https://openbadges.org/about/

15 Jeffrey R. Young, "Why Udacity and EdX want to trademark the degrees of the future—and what's at stake for students," EdSurge, November 3, 2016. https://www.edsurge.com/news/2016-11-03-why-udacity-and-edx-want-to-trademark-the-degrees-of-the-future-and-what-s-at-stake-for-students

16 "Discussion Paper: Review of the Australian Qualifications Framework," Australian Department of Education and Training, December 2018. https://docs.education.gov.au/node/51926

17 Anne-Marie Slaughter, "Care Is as Important as Career," *TIME*, May 6, 2016. https://time.com/4321549/anne-marie-slaughter-university-of-utah-commencement-speech/

Chapter 5

1   Caged Bird Legacy homepage. https://www.mayaangelou.com/

2   Lumina Foundation, "Apprenticeship program an Rx for CVS workers' success," *Focus*: "Investing wisely" Spring 2018, 22–28.

3   "The American Skills Gap is Real," Adecco, October 22, 2019. https://www.adeccousa.com/employers/resources/skills-gap-in-the-american-workforce/

4   "Today's Student," Lumina Foundation, 2019. https://www.luminafoundation.org/campaign/todays-student/

5   Department for Education and Anne Milton, "Key facts you should know about the apprenticeship levy," gov.uk, April 5, 2019. https://www.gov.uk/government/news/key-facts-you-should-know-about-the-apprenticeship-levy

6   "Registered Apprenticeship National Results for FY 2018," U.S. Department of Labor. https://www.doleta.gov/OA/data_statistics.cfm

7   Bundesinstitut für Berufsbildung (BIBB), VET data report for Germany, 2017.

8   Lumina Foundation, "If you have employees who are bright ... why not train them?" *Focus*: "Not tardy ... timely" Fall 2017, 31–33.

9   "Higher apprenticeships," The Apprenticeship Guide. http://www.apprenticeshipguide.co.uk/higher-apprenticeships/

10 The Imperative of Higher Apprenticeships, Australian Industry Group, July 2018.

11 The Australian report cited above calls U.S. efforts to develop higher and degree apprenticeships "piecemeal."

12 "It's Time: Using Modern Apprenticeships to Reskill America," IWSI
    America, 2019. https://www.iwsiamerica.org/itstime/
13 American Staffing Association Workforce Monitor poll conducted by
    Harris, 2018.
14 Ibid.
15 Vivian Giang, "This company uses AI to test unlikely engineers for
    their potential," *Fast Company*, November 30, 2018. https://www.
    fastcompany.com/90269298/this-company-uses-ai-to-test-unlikely-
    engineers-for-their-potential
16 John Hagel III and John Seely Brown, "Great Businesses Scale Their
    Learning, Not Just Their Operations," *Harvard Business Review*, June
    7, 2017. https://hbr.org/2017/06/great-businesses-scale-their-learning-not-
    just-their-operations
17 https://www.luminafoundation.org/resources/?type=1019/
18 "Talent Investments Pay Off," Lumina Foundation. https://www.
    luminafoundation.org/files/resources/discover-roi-executive-briefing.pdf
19 Seymour's place in the global supply chain for diesel engines could be
    threatened by trade disputes. As CEO Tom Linebarger put it in a *New
    York Times* article, "The existence of this plant is a direct result of our
    company's ability to access global markets." Tom Linebarger, "A message
    from a CEO: Tarrifs are going to hurt American companies," *New York
    Times*, July 25, 2018. https://www.nytimes.com/2018/07/25/opinion/
    trump-tariffs-hurt-manufacturing-jobs.html
20 Mary Titsworth Chandler, "Cummins Inc.: Partnering to Provide
    Technical Education for Communities," Global Business Coalition for
    Education, December 3, 2013. https://gbc-education.org/cummins-inc-
    partnering-to-provide-technical-education-for-communities/
21 One hundred percent of Cummins workers in India and 95% in China
    participated in community service in 2016. Blair Claiflin, "Cummins
    Employees Continue Engaging In Big Numbers to Build Stronger
    Communities," Cummins, March 1, 2017. https://www.cummins.com/
    news/2017/03/01/cummins-employees-continue-engaging-big-numbers-
    build-stronger-communities
22 As to the way academe sees service, this article is worth reading:
    Anonymous, "My journey with department service," Inside Higher Ed,
    February 2, 2018.https://www.insidehighered.com/advice/2018/02/02/
    costs-minorities-performing-service-work-academe-opinion

Chapter 6

1   Karsten Paul and Klaus Moser, "Unemployment impairs mental health:
    Meta-analyses," *Journal of Vocational Behavior*, Vol. 74, No. 3, June
    2009, pp. 264–282.

2   A.H. Winefield, M. Tiggemann, H.R. Winefield, and R.D. Goldney, "Social Alienation and Employment Status in Young Adults," *Journal of Organizational Behavior*, Vol. 12, No. 2, March 1991, pp. 145–154.

3   David Graeber, *Bullshit Jobs: A Theory*, Simon & Schuster, May 2018.

4   David H. Autor, "Work of the Past, Work of the Future," *AEA Papers and Proceedings 2019*, Vol. 109, pp. 1–32. https://doi.org/10.1257/pandp.20191110

5   Eduardo Porter, "Tech Is Splitting the U.S. Work Force in Two," *New York Times*, February 4, 2019. https://www.nytimes.com/2019/02/04/business/economy/productivity-inequality-wages.html

6   Carl Benedikt Frey, Thor Berger, and Chinchih Chen, "Political machinery: did robots swing the 2016 U.S. presidential election?" *Oxford Review of Economic Policy*, Vol. 34, No. 3, Autumn 2018, pp. 418–442.

7   Bruce Katz, "Red State/Blue City Isn't the Whole Story," *Bloomberg CityLab*, March 13, 2017. https://www.citylab.com/equity/2017/03/red-stateblue-city-isnt-the-whole-story/519306/

8   Mark Muro, Jacob Whiton, and Robert Maxim, "Automation perpetuates the red-blue divide," Brookings, March 19, 2019. https://www.brookings.edu/blog/the-avenue/2019/03/25/automation-perpetuates-the-red-blue-divide/

9   A plan for restoring local journalism can be found in "Losing the News: The Decimation of Local News and the Search for Solutions," PEN America, November 20, 2019. https://pen.org/local-news/

10 "Measles cases spike globally due to gaps in vaccination coverage," World Health Organization, November 29, 2018. https://www.who.int/news-room/detail/29-11-2018-measles-cases-spike-globally-due-to-gaps-in-vaccination-coverage

11 Laura Paisley, "Political polarization at its worst since the Civil War," *USC News*, November 8, 2016. https://news.usc.edu/110124/political-polarization-at-its-worst-since-the-civil-war-2/

12 Twenty-three percent of Democrats and 10% of Republicans. Jason Szep, "'Go to hell!' A divided America struggles to heal after ugly election," *Reuters*, November 9, 2016. https://www.reuters.com/article/us-usa-election-division-insight-idUSKBN13419A

13 Anjana Susarla, "The new digital divide is between people who opt out of algorithms and people who don't," *The Conversation*, April 17, 2019. https://theconversation.com/the-new-digital-divide-is-between-people-who-opt-out-of-algorithms-and-people-who-dont-114719

14 The discussion of authoritarianism in this section draws from research conducted by the Georgetown University Center on Education and the Workforce; see Anthony P. Carnevale, Nicole Smith, Lenka Dražanová, Artem Gulish, and Kathryn Peltier Campbell, "The Role of Education in Taming Authoritarian Attitudes," Georgetown University Center on Education and the Workforce, Washington, D.C., forthcoming.

15 Karen Stenner, *The Authoritarian Dynamic*, Cambridge University Press, 2005, p. 81, as cited by Carnevale et al., forthcoming.

16 Howard Sanborn and Clayton L. Thyne, "Learning Democracy: Education and the Fall of Authoritarian Regimes," *British Journal of Political Science*, 2013.

17 Anthony P. Carnevale, et al., "The Role of Education."

18 Lee Drutman, Larry Diamond, and Joe Goldman, "Follow the Leader: Exploring American Support for Democracy and Authoritarianism," Democracy Fund Voter Study Group, March 2018. https://www. voterstudygroup.org/publication/follow-the-leader

19 Richard Wike, Katie Simmons, Bruce Stokes, and Janell Fetterolf, "Globally, Broad Support for Representative and Direct Democracy," Pew Research Center, October 16, 2017. https://www.pewresearch. org/global/2017/10/16/globally-broad-support-for-representative-and-direct-democracy/

20 J.W. Prothro and C.M. Grigg, "Fundamental Principles of Democracy," *Journal of Politics*, Vol. 22, No. 2, May 1960, pp. 276–294; Herbert McClosky, "Consensus and Ideology in American Politics," *American Political Science Review*, Vol. 58, No. 2, June 1964, pp. 361–382.

21 Georgetown University Center on Education and the Workforce regression analysis of data from the General Social Survey, 1986–2016, and the American National Election Studies, 2000–2016.

22 Voter Turnout Demographics, Unites States Election Project. http://www. electproject.org/home/voter-turnout/demographics

23 Volunteering in the United States 2015, Bureau of Labor Statistics.

24 David E. Campbell, "What is education's impact on civic and social engagement?" OECD, 2006.

25 http://www.worldvaluessurvey.org/WVSEventsShow.jsp?ID=255

26 Anthony P. Carnevale, "We Need a New Deal Between Higher Education and Democratic Capitalism," Georgetown University Center on Education and the Workforce, 2016. https://cew.georgetown.edu/wp-content/ uploads/new-deal.pdf

27 Justin McCarthy, "About Half of Americans Say U.S. Moral Values Are 'Poor.'" Gallup, June 1, 2018.

28 Inquiry and analysis VALUE rubric, Association of American Colleges and Universities, 2009. https://www.aacu.org/value/rubrics/inquiry-analysis

29 Final Report National Geographic–Roper Public Affairs Geographic Literacy Study, 2006.

30 Lucy Williamson, "France's Macron brings back national service," *BBC*, June 27, 2018. https://www.bbc.com/news/world-europe-44625625

31 National Citizen Service 2016 Evaluation Main Report.

32 Amy McGarvey, Véronique Jochum, John Davies, Joy Dobbs and Lisa Hornung, "Time well spent: A national survey on the volunteer experience," NCVO, January 2019. https://www.ncvo.org.uk/images/

documents/policy_and_research/volunteering/Volunteer-experience_
Full-Report.pdf

33 "Virgil D. Hawkins story," UF Law. https://www.law.ufl.edu/areas-of-
study/experiential-learning/clinics/virgil-d-hawkins-story

Conclusion

1   Jamie Merisotis, "The Leadership Model of Philanthropy," Lumina
Foundation. https://www.luminafoundation.org/files/resources/leadership-
model-of-philanthropy.pdf

Index

Page numbers in *italics* refer to figures and tables.

About the Author

Jamie Merisotis is a globally recognized leader in philanthropy, education, and public policy. Since 2008, he has served as president and CEO of Lumina Foundation, an independent, private foundation that is committed to making opportunities for learning beyond high school available to all. He previously served as co-founder and president of the nonpartisan, Washington, D.C.–based Institute for Higher Education Policy and as executive director of a bipartisan national commission on college affordability appointed by the U.S. president and congressional leaders. Merisotis is the author of *America Needs Talent*, which was named a Top 10 Business Book of 2016 by *Booklist*, a publication of the American Library Association.

Merisotis is a frequent media commentator and contributor. His writing has appeared in the *New York Times*, the *Wall Street Journal*, the *Washington Post*, *National Journal*, *Stanford Social Innovation Review*, *Politico*, *Roll Call*, *Washington Monthly*, and other publications.

His work includes experience as an advisor and consultant in southern Africa, the former Soviet Union, Europe, and other parts of the world. A respected analyst and innovator, Merisotis is a member of the Council on Foreign Relations in New York. Merisotis serves as chairman of the Council on Foundations in

Washington, D.C., and past chairman of The Children's Museum of Indianapolis, the world's largest museum for children. He also serves on the boards of the Central Indiana Corporate Partnership and the United Kingdom–based European Access Network. He lives with his wife Colleen O'Brien and their children, Benjamin and Elizabeth, in Indianapolis.